BRIDGE OVER TROUBLED BIDDING

JAN PITTELLI

ISBN: 1466476613
ISBN 13: 9781466476615

I dedicate this book to my students who work so hard at mastering this game and to my husband for his help and support these past 50 years. Thank you Joe.

TABLE OF CONTENTS

INTRODUCTION

Have you ever bought a book on Bridge and after making a couple of attempts to read it left it on the bookshelf to collect dust? Perhaps you started Bridge classes, but couldn't get a good feel for the basics. Chances are you dropped out feeling very discouraged. Many people become so discouraged during the initial learning period that they lose interest, and often times even those who remain struggle for a long time.

Bridge has the reputation of being a very difficult game. Try suggesting Bridge lessons to your friends, and you are sure to hear, "I don't have time," "It's too serious" or "It involves too much work." There seems to be an endless number of reasons not to give the game a try.

Although Bridge could never be described as easy, it certainly isn't as difficult as its reputation leads us to believe. This reputation has been acquired because, too often, Bridge is approached as if today's new player will be playing in tomorrow's World Championships. Players taking their first class or opening their first Bridge book are barraged with a multitude of bidding procedures and playing techniques.

Even learning "hands on" from experienced players has its drawbacks. Experienced players are anxious to demonstrate their knowledge and command of the game, and - instead of concentrating on the fundamentals -they begin teaching the rare bids and exceptions. This can be overwhelming to someone just trying to grasp the basics.

Is it possible to approach Bridge without suffering all this discouragement and frustration? Yes. It can be done by building a solid foundation before tackling more complicated and advanced techniques. In fact, if you conquer the basics, you will be able to play a very respectable game of bridge even if you elect not to use the more advanced techniques.

Helping you build that strong foundation is what this book is all about. It is designed for the beginner, but any player interested in updating and upgrading his or her bidding skills will find it beneficial.

After you have established a solid foundation, you will then be ready to seek a greater knowledge of the game. Inch by inch, there is more to understand and appreciate. Bridge may be difficult but it is never boring, and as your knowledge grows, so will your enjoyment of the game. With time, effort and patience, you can have a lifetime of fun, good fellowship and intellectual stimulation.

This game commands respect. It is the world's most interesting, fascinating and popular card game. Right from the start, be aware that it is going to take time and effort to become proficient at Bridge. If you are a person who requires immediate gratification, perhaps you should consider another pastime -- you simply cannot absorb all there is to learn in a short period of time.

It is best to think of learning Bridge as a lifetime endeavor. Each time you play, for as long as you play, there will be something new and interesting to learn. That is the beauty of the game; you need to take lessons, read, study and practice to become a really good player. But if you are patient and willing to put forth the necessary effort, it will be a very rewarding experience.

Before turning our attention to the game itself, here are a few suggestions to help you approach Bridge without the usual apprehension. Be aware that you will be learning a lot of new information and trying to use it correctly. As in any new endeavor, errors - and plenty of them - are going to be made.

When children try something new, they make mistakes, but they have the wonderful ability to pick themselves up, dust themselves off, and start all over again. Unfortunately, as we grow older, we protect ourselves from embarrassment; we are afraid of looking stupid or making fools of ourselves. Learning Bridge is going to be more difficult if you allow yourself to be overcome with embarrassment or fear. Remember, no one is perfect, especially a beginning Bridge player. From the start, give yourself permission to make mistakes. Take comfort in the fact that we all make mistakes but we learn from our mistakes.

Bridge players are notorious for offering advice to new players. When this happens, try not to think of it as criticism. More often than not, it is given out of interest in the game rather than to single out a particular player. If you have trouble viewing advice as anything other than criticism, learn to accept input as a teaching tool rather than as a personal attack.

Of course, all Bridge players are not perfect human beings. Occasionally, you'll run into a very critical know-it-all type of player. While building this foundation, avoid such personalities. Hypercritical people can make you feel embarrassed and self-conscious, and hinder your progress. You need self-confidence to cope with them and building that confidence is the goal of this book.

There are many levels of competition available to Bridge players. Most people are interested in playing socially, and playing well enough to feel comfortable at the Bridge table. Many Bridge lovers remain social players all their lives, while others become more involved in the game, and eventually seek out competitive groups. Which path you will follow remains to be seen, but let's get started.

THE GAME

T he only requirements for a game of Bridge are four players, a deck of regular playing cards (no jokers), paper, pencil and a table with four chairs. Well, maybe you should add an open mind to that list.

Success at the Bridge table requires luck and skill. Both play an important role. Luck you can't change or control, but your level of skill can improve dramatically if you practice bidding and playing techniques. There is one other factor to consider, and that is communication. This is a partnership game and communication with your partner is as important as luck and skill combined. Cooperation, communication and respect for your partner are the keys to success. Always think of your partnership as a team, and of teamwork as your most important asset. Good communication with your partner keeps Lady Luck smiling over your shoulder.

Partnerships may be prearranged or chosen by having each of the four players draw a card from a deck of cards. The Ace is the highest card, then the King, Queen, Jack, ten, nine, etc., down to the two. The pair drawing the two highest cards is one partnership, and the remaining pair is the other partnership. Partners sit opposite each other at the table, and are referred to as compass positions; North and South compete against East and West. There is no advantage to sitting in any one of the four directions. The simplest way to determine where each player sits is to decide who is North, and place his partner, South, across the table from him. After that, East and West should be easy.

Once the partnerships have been determined, draw cards again. The player drawing the highest card is the first DEALER. The dealer shuffles the cards, asks his right-hand opponent (RHO) to cut the deck, and distributes or DEALS the cards. The cards are dealt face down, one at a time. The first card is dealt to the dealer's left-hand opponent (LHO) and the deal continues in a clockwise rotation until all 52 cards have been dealt. When the deal is complete, the players pick up their HANDS and sort them into SUITS. The suits are Clubs, Diamonds, Hearts and Spades. Hearts and Spades are called MAJOR SUITS; Clubs and Diamonds are the MINOR SUITS.

The object of the game is to win TRICKS. A trick is a unit of play that begins when one player leads a card (you will learn how to select the player who leads to each trick)and ends when the other three players have played a card to it. These four cards make up one trick. There is a winner for each trick. Each player is dealt 13 cards, and it follows that a hand of Bridge has 13 tricks.

The Two Stages Of The Game Of Bridge

1. THE BIDDING STAGE

The game begins with the players bidding in an AUCTION. Each bid is a promise to take a certain number of tricks. The partnership bidding to take the most tricks enters into a CONTRACT to take the number of tricks they bid.

2. THE PLAYING STAGE

After the auction, the hand is played. The partnership winning the contract tries to win enough tricks to fulfill their contract and the other partnership tries to prevent them from doing so.

SUIT AND NOTRUMP CONTRACTS

The hand may be played in a SUIT CONTRACT or in a NOTRUMP CONTRACT. In a suit contract, one of the suits (Clubs, Diamonds, Hearts, Spades) is designated as "special". This special suit is called TRUMP. All cards in the trump suit are given added power for the entire hand. In a Notrump contract, there is no special or trump suit. The partnership buying the contract decides if the hand is played with a trump suit with a particular suit as trump or if it will be played without a trump suit in a Notrump contract. Therefore, the hand can be played in one of five possibilities – Clubs, Diamonds, Hearts, Spades, or Notrump. These possibilities are called STRAINS.

In both Notrump and trump contracts, you must – if you have one– play a card of the suit led. This is called FOLLOWING SUIT. If you have no cards in the suit led, you can DISCARD from another suit. In a Notrump contract, the highest card of the suit led always wins the trick. In a suit contract, it may be possible to use the power of the trump suit to win a trick. If you can't follow suit, you have the option of discarding or playing a trump card (called trumping or ruffing). A trump card beats any card from a non-trump suit. The lowly two of trump beats the Ace of a non-trump suit. A trump card can only be beaten by a higher trump card.

In some card games, you must lead or play trump at specified times. Not so in bridge. If a hand is played in a trump contract, the decision of when to lead or play a trump is up to the individual player. However, if a trump is led, you must follow suit. It may seem strange not to play a trump when you could, but it is not always necessary. For example, if it is your turn to play to a trick and you hold no cards in the suit led, you have the choice of discarding or trumping. If your partner's high card is going to win the trick, there is no need for your partnership to win the trick twice. In a situation such as this, you would choose to discard rather than waste a trump. Remember, this is a partnership game.

DECLARER
AND DUMMY

After the bidding stage is over, the hand is played. The player of the winning partnership who first mentioned the STRAIN of the final contract (Clubs, Diamonds, Hearts, Spades, Notrump) plays the hand and is called the DECLARER. To illustrate, if the final contract is in Spades, the player who bid Spades first is the declarer. His partner does not participate in the play of the hand and is called the DUMMY. This sounds like a cruel term, but that is how the game is played. Don't take it personally.

The player to the left of the declarer always begins the playing stage by leading the first card. He does this by placing his chosen card face up on the table. He is making the OPENING LEAD. After the opening lead, the dummy places all his cards face up on the table in columns of suits. If there is a trump suit, it is placed in the column to the dummy's right. This hand is referred to as DUMMY(or the board) for the remainder of the hand. Remember, the declarer's partner (dummy) does not play any cards and is strictly an observer. He does not assist the declarer in the play of the hand.

Beginning with the hand to the left of the opening leader and continuing in clockwise rotation, each player plays a card on the opening lead. The declarer plays, in turn, a card from the dummy and a card from his hand. After each player has contributed a card, these four cards constitute the first TRICK of the hand. If no trump cards were placed on the trick, the highest card of the suit led wins. If there were trumps played to the trick, the highest trump card wins. The winner of that trick leads the next card. This continues until all 13 tricks have been played.

The declarer's goal is to make enough tricks to fulfill his bidding contract. His partnership is awarded points if he takes the number of tricks promised in his contract. The other two players defend the hand and are called the DEFENDERS. The goal of the defenders is to prevent the declarer from taking enough tricks to fulfill his contract because in doing so, they score points. While playing the hand, the declarer keeps track of his winning tricks, and the defenders keep track of the number of tricks they win. After the hand is played, the tricks are counted. If the declarer wins the number of tricks in his contract, he is awarded points. If he falls short of the required number, the defenders are awarded points.

While learning the basics of bidding, try not to worry about how the game is scored. You will learn how to score as you go along. Experienced players would much rather play with a novice who has an understanding of bidding rather than scoring. They will be happy to keep score.

After the hand has been scored, the next hand is dealt. The dealer for the next hand is always the player to the left of the previous dealer.

THE GOAL OF THE BIDDING STAGE IS TO BID THE BEST CONTRACT FOR YOUR PARTNERSHIP'S COMBINED HANDS. THE GOAL OF THE PLAYING STAGE IS TO MAKE THE CONTRACT YOU BID.

THE BIDDING AUCTION

Each stage of the learning process requires special knowledge and skills, and must be looked at separately. The objective of this book is to help you build a solid foundation in bidding and only addresses the bidding stage of the game. It was designed to simplify and make the basic bidding techniques as clear as possible. The basic principles of bidding are explained and nothing tricky about the bidding system is included. This is strictly STANDARD AMERICAN BRIDGE presented in a way that hopefully makes it easier to understand.

After you have completed this book and done the exercises, you will be capable of handling the bidding necessary for the types of hands you encounter most of the time. You have heard the old saying, "You must learn to crawl before you can walk." This is certainly true in Bridge. After learning the bidding skills necessary for the most common types of hands, you can then add advanced techniques for those you seldom or rarely see. Unusual hands are fun to bid and play, but they must wait until you have a solid foundation in the basics.

Years of experience have proven that a solid foundation in basic bidding is the most important part of the bidding process. Do not be anxious to add advanced techniques to your game. They will not help you as much as basic principles. If you have a good grasp of the basics and you and your partner elect not to add more advanced techniques to your game, you will still be able to play a good game of bridge.

The auction goes like this: The dealer has the first bidding opportunity in the auction. He may either make a BID (sometimes referred to as a CALL) or he may say PASS. A bid or a call is a promise to take a certain number of tricks. When a player passes, he does not want to make a bid on that particular round of bidding. Whether the dealer makes a bid or passes, the player to his left has the next opportunity to make a bid. Each of the four players has the opportunity to bid on the first round but after on the next rounds, the bidding ends when there are three passes in a row. Just like a regular auction, going, going, gone. If you pass on one of your turns to bid, you are not barred from entering the auction at a later turn. You may bid as long as there have not been three passes in a row.

BRIDGE LINGO

A bid is a player's promise to take a certain number of tricks, but it is also a way to give his partner information or ask him a question. During the bidding process, much information can be exchanged even though the bidding vocabulary consists of only 15 words. These words are one, two, three, four, five, six, seven, Clubs, Diamonds, Hearts, Spades, Notrump, double, redouble and pass. Combinations of these words take on different meanings, depending on the player who is speaking and the stage of the auction. This is the language of Bridge. The more fluent you and your partner become in this language, the more success you will have. You'll be learning how to determine the meanings as you progress in the book. For now, just be aware these words and only these words may be used and when used correctly, your partnership can reach a good contract.

It would be advantageous to practice the exercises with a potential partner. An even better idea is to practice with several potential partners. Having more than one player with whom you can communicate is a real bonanza. When doing the exercises, it is a good idea to practice with one person asking the questions while the others try to answer correctly. Players are encouraged to discuss how the questions should be answered before doing so. A lively discussion is always a good way to learn.

UNDERSTANDING BIDDING LEVELS

There are 13 tricks in a hand of Bridge. When you enter the bidding, you are saying you can take more tricks than your opponents. This means you must take more than six tricks. Therefore, six tricks are automatically included in each bid and are referred to as BOOK. When you make a bid, you are saying you can take more tricks than BOOK. The number you bid will say how many tricks you are willing to bid over six. There are 13 total tricks in a hand of bridge so your bids will be from one to seven.

The remaining seven tricks are placed on a BIDDING SCALE and are called BIDDING LEVELS. The bidding scale starts at the one level and ends at the seven level. Each level promises a certain number of tricks over book. A bid at the one level promises one trick over book or seven tricks. A bid at the three level promises three tricks over book or nine tricks. A bid at the seven level, promises all 13 tricks. To determine how many tricks you need to take to make your bid, add six to the level of your bid.

RANKING THE SUITS

Each bid not only contains a level (one to seven) but also a strain (Clubs, Diamonds, Hearts, Spades, Notrump). For bidding purposes, the strains are ranked on each level with Clubs as the lowest, then Diamonds, then Hearts, then Spades, then Notrump. It is easy to remember how the suits are ranked because ranking of the suits is done in alphabetical order C-D-H-S, and Notrump is always at the top of each level.

Think of the bidding scale as a staircase. You begin at the bottom (1Club) and move up. In order to make a bid, you must climb higher on the staircase than the last bidder. For example, 1Diamond outbids 1Club, but 1Heart outbids 1Diamond. One Notrump outbids all the one-level suits, but 2Clubs outbids 1Notrump.

Keep this bidding scale handy when you are learning how to bid. The smallest bid on the scale is 1Club and the bids go upward to the top, which is 7 Notrump.

THE BIDDING SCALE

7 Notrump
7 Spades
7 Hearts
7 Diamonds
7 Clubs
6 Notrump
6 Spades
6 Hearts
6 Diamonds
6 Clubs
5 Notrump
5 Spades
5 Hearts
5 Diamonds
5 Clubs
4 Notrump
4 Spades
4 Hearts
4 Diamonds
4 Clubs
3 Notrump
3 Spades
3 Hearts
3 Diamonds
3 Clubs
2 Notrump
2 Spades
2 Hearts
2 Diamonds
2 Clubs
1 Notrump
1 Spade
1 Heart
1 Diamond
1 Club

DECIDING WHAT
IS TRUMP

You enter into the auction hoping to buy the contract, but you are also looking for a good trump suit. Through teamwork and communication, your partnership searches for a trump suit that is best for your combined hands. This suit may not be your favorite suit, but that is unimportant. You are not competing against your partner to name the suit you like best as trump. Instead, you are cooperating to find a trump suit that is best for your partnership. Teamwork.

To declare a suit as trump, your partnership needs to have more cards in the suit than your opponents have. There are 13 cards in each suit. To have the majority of a suit, you must have at least seven cards of that suit in your combined hands. With seven or more cards, you are said to have a FIT. It is called a fit because your two hands blend or fit together to hold the majority of cards in that suit. Sometimes, you play a seven-card fit as a trump suit but it is not considered a strong trump fit. You'll want your trump fit to be stronger. A fit of at least eight cards constitutes a strong trump fit and that is what you are hoping to find. How these cards are divided between your hand and your partner's hand is unimportant. They may be divided 7-1, 6-2, 5-3, 4-4 or even 8-0. As long as your partnership has a total of eight cards, it doesn't matter how they are divided.

Are you asking yourself, "How on earth am I supposed to know if my partner and I have eight or more cards in a particular suit?" That is what the bidding auction is all about. You and your partner use Bridge language to tell each other about the number of cards you hold in your suits. You don't need to know how to do this just yet, and (have no fear) you will be given plenty of help when the time comes. For now, it is only important to know that finding an eight-card fit is your goal.

UNDERSTANDING SPLITS

There are two reasons a partnership wants to have an eight-card trump fit. The first and obvious reason is you have more than a minimum majority of cards in that suit. The second and more important reason has to do with how your opponents' cards in that suit will divide. If your partnership has eight cards of a particular suit, your opponents have the remaining five. How those five cards divide between your two opponents is called the SPLIT. When naming a trump suit, you want their cards to split so neither opponent has more than three trump cards.

How a certain number of outstanding cards should split has been mathematically calculated and is very predictable. An odd number of cards usually divides as evenly as possible, and an even number of cards usually divides slightly unevenly. The mathematically predicted splits are:

PREDICTED SPLITS

Number of cards you and your partner hold	Number of cards opponents hold between their hands	Likely Splits
7	6	4 and 2
8	5	3 and 2
9	4	3 and 1
10	3	2 and 1

Look at the Predicted Splits chart. If your partnership holds a minimum of eight cards in a suit, the odds are in your favor that the outstanding cards will split or divide between your opponents so that neither will have more than three. This is called a FAVORABLE SPLIT. Selection of a trump suit is based on these predicted splits.

Are you now wondering why you don't want either opponent to hold more than three trump cards? When the hand is played, you don't want the opponents to trump your winners in the non-trump suits. To prevent this, you usually draw trump (lead the trump suit) as soon as possible and continue to draw it until both opponents have been exhausted of their trump supply. Look at the predicted splits chart. Can you see that with a trump fit of eight or more cards, you need to lead trump only three times because neither of the opponents is likely to have more than three trump cards? After drawing three rounds of the trump suit, your winners in the non-trump suits are safe because neither opponent will have any trumps left. Your remaining trump cards can then be used to trump losers in the non-trump suits.

There are many expressions unique to Bridge. Drawing the trump from your opponents' hands is called GETTING THE KIDDIES OFF THE STREET. You hear expressions such as this one when you play the game, and it is good to know what they mean.

Look at the Predicted Splits chart one more time. Notice that when your partnership has only a seven-card fit, there are six cards out against you. The predicted split is four cards in one opponent's hand and two cards in the other. To pull all the trump, you must lead the trump suit four times. This reduces the number of trump cards you will have for trumping losers in non-trump suits, and increases the likelihood of the opponents trumping one of your non-trump winners. Can you see why a seven-card fit is a weaker trump fit?

Although selection of the trump suit is based on mathematically predicted splits, you must understand that the game is also part luck. A favorable split is what you hope for and usually get, but occasionally, Lady Luck hands you a raw deal and the opponents' cards split unfavorably. This is possible even when you have a fit of eight or more cards. Bridge, like life, isn't always perfect, but if you bet on what happens most of the time, you'll come out ahead in the game.

EXERCISES

1. What is a fit?
   Answer: When you and your partner hold seven or more cards in a suit.

2. Why are you looking for a fit of eight or more cards?
   Answer: You have a comfortable majority and the opponents' cards usually split favorably. You probably won't have to draw trump more than three times.

3. What is the most likely split with an even number of cards?
   Answer: They will usually divide slightly unevenly.

4. What is the most likely split with an odd number of cards?
   Answer: They will usually divide as evenly as possible.

FACE CARD HANGUP

Your partnership is looking for a strong fit of eight or more cards. This may sound unbelievable, but an eight-card fit makes a strong trump fit with or without FACE

CARDS (Aces, Kings, Queens, Jacks). This is not a new concept invented by this author. A trump fit of eight or more cards has always been the goal of Bridge players.

Many players envision a trump suit loaded with face cards. Let's call this FACE CARD HANG-UP. Face Card Hang-Up causes trouble and confusion and is one of the biggest stumbling blocks to good bidding. Always keep in mind, when you open the bidding in a suit or you are responding to an opening bid, you are suggesting the suit you bid as a trump suit, but you are not promising high card strength in that suit. You are simply promising a minimum number of cards in that suit. What cards they happen to be is unimportant.

Face Card Hang-Up has its roots in fear – the fear of losing tricks. Players fear losing tricks and for some reason, losing tricks in the trump suit is particularly frightening. Think of Bridge as a game of winning tricks and losing tricks. You rarely win all 13 tricks. You are almost certainly going to lose some tricks and if you lose those tricks in the trump suit, so be it. A loser in the trump suit loses exactly one trick, the same as any non-trump loser.

Don't assume that all experienced players are bidding correctly. Many have been playing for years with a full blown case of Face Card Hang-Up. Although your spouse or Aunt Helen may have different ideas regarding the bidding process, as a beginning Bridge player, it is best to learn correct bidding techniques. Most importantly, have a partner who agrees that an eight-card fit (any cards) is the primary goal in the search for a trump suit. Once again, communication is the key to success.

REVIEW

1. If you and your partner have the majority of the cards in a suit (at least seven), you are said to have a fit.
2. With eight or more cards in suit between you and your partner, you have a strong fit.
3. To declare a suit as trump, you want a strong fit of at least eight cards.
4. These eight cards may be any cards in the suit.
5. Don't become preoccupied with having face cards in your trump suit. They have little impact on the strength of your trump fit.
6. With eight or more cards between you, your partnership has an adequate majority and usually gets a favorable split of the opponents' cards. Your cards may be divided between you and your partner 8-0, 7-1, 6-2, 5-3, or 4-4.
7. You usually need to draw trump no more than three times with five cards or less out against you.
8. Mathematically predicted splits aren't guaranteed, but with an eight card or longer fit, the odds are with you.

EXERCISES

1. Does your trump suit need to be loaded with face cards?
   Answer: NO, NO, NO.

2. When a player believes the trump suit should be loaded with face cards, what does this author call this affliction?

Answer: Face Card Hang-up.

3. What are the keys to success in a Bridge partnership?

Answer: Communication, Communication, Communication

DETERMINING
THE VALUE
OF YOUR HAND

Now that you know a bid consists of a level and either a particular suit or Notrump and you are hoping to find an eight-card trump fit, how do you know if your hand is strong enough to open the bidding (be the first player to bid something other than pass)?   There are features in your hand that have the potential to take tricks. These features are FACE CARDS (Aces, Kings, Queens, Jacks) and LONG SUITS. A long suit is a suit with five or more cards. To determine the strength of your hand, these features are rated on a point scale of one to four according to how likely they are to take a trick. The total of these points is the point value of your hand.

HAND VALUATION

FACE CARD VALUATION

Ace (very likely to take a trick)................. 4 points
King (second most likely to take a trick) ... 3 points
Queen (somewhat likely) .... 2 points
Jack (not very likely) .... 1 point

These points are called HIGH CARD POINTS (HCP's).

It is easy to see the trick-taking possibilities of face cards, but LONG CARDS (cards over four in length) can also take tricks. After a suit has been led several times, you may be the only player with any cards left in the suit. These cards become winners even if they are small because your opponents have none left to beat them. Because there is a possibility of winning tricks with your long cards, they are also given a point value. They have about the same likelihood of taking a trick as a Jack. Therefore, one point each is given for the fifth, sixth, seventh, eighth, etc. cards in all of your long suits.

LONG CARD VALUATION

5 card suit.....................1 point (one long card)
6 card suit.....................2 points (2 long cards)
7 card suit.....................3 points (3 long cards)
8 card suit.....................4 points (4 long cards), etc.

These are called DISTRIBUTION POINTS OR LONG CARD POINTS.

Add all your high card points to your long card points and you have the total point count of your hand. Use this method to value your hand and do not combine it with any methods you may have used previously. Great care should be taken to make sure you have counted and added correctly. Know that a single point can make a big difference in what you bid. Never think, "I have about (or around) 13 points." Either you have exactly 13 points or you have something else. There is nothing complicated about counting your points, and your total point count is calculated by simple addition. No one but you can count and add your points. You can do it easily and while you are doing it, do it correctly!

Your partner wants to know your total number of points. The bids you make promise not only a minimum number of cards in the suits you bid (we will get to that next), but also a certain number of points in your hand. The combined count of your total points and your partner's total points determine how high your partnership should bid on the bidding scale. If you are a person who always needs something to worry about, worry about counting your points correctly.

Face Card Hang-Up has a way of taking over. Players are blinded by face cards and somehow neglect the importance of counting correctly. Your partner, however, is interested in your total point count. He does not care if the points come from Aces, Kings, Queens, Jacks or long cards.

Let's use an example of buying a ninety nine cent chocolate bar. Remember the last time you had a chocolate craving and desperately wanted to buy a chocolate bar.....but didn't have enough money? You may have asked a friend to help you. Did it matter how the two of you came up with the money? Did it really matter if it was in pennies, nickels, dimes or quarters? No, what coins made up the total or which pockets you took them from was irrelevant. What was important was you had the ninety nine cents and could buy the candy bar.

Back to Bridge. To buy a particular contract, the experts recommend you have a certain number of combined points. For example, to buy a contract at the four level, say 4 Spades, 25 points are necessary. They only stipulate 25 points. Nowhere is it written you need so many Aces, Kings, Queens, Jacks, or long cards. They do not mention which suits must contain the points or that the points must be in the suits you bid. You and your partner need a TOTAL of 25 points. Count your face card points along with your long card points and concern yourself only with obtaining an accurate total.

REVIEW

1. Value your hand count High Card Points.
   Aces - 4, Kings - 3, Queens - 2, Jacks - 1

2. Give value to your long suits (five card or longer). Add one point each for the fifth, sixth, seventh, eighth card etc. in any and all long suits.

3. The importance of a correct point count can not be stressed strongly enough.

EXERCISE

Deal some hands with a regular deck of cards and count the number of total points for each hand. There is nothing difficult about this, it is simple addition. When you have determined the value for each hand and you are sure you are counting correctly, redeal and do it again. Continue doing this until you are very confident. It is best to practice with another player so the two of you can check on each other.

DETERMINING
THE SHAPE
OF YOUR HAND

After you have counted your points, there is one more chore before bidding. The SHAPE of your hand must be determined. To make this determination, it is necessary to know the meaning of these three words:

VOID....................You have no cards in a suit.
SINGLETON.........You have only one card in a suit.
DOUBLETON.......You have only two cards in a suit.

A hand has one of two shapes. It is either BALANCED or it is UNBALANCED. A balanced hand contains no voids, no singletons, and no more than one doubleton. If a hand contains a void, a singleton, or more than one doubleton, it is unbalanced. It is never "kinda" or "sorta" balanced. Think of a balanced hand as being pregnant: Either your hand is balanced or it is not. The only balanced hands are hands with these distributions (it makes no difference which suits hold which cards).

XXXX	XXXX	XXXXX
XXX	XXXX	XXX
XXX	XXX	XXX
XXX	XX	XX
4-3-3-3	4-4-3-2	5-3-3-2
4 cards in 1 suit	4 cards in 2 suits	5 cards in 1 suit
3 cards in all other suits	3 cards in 1 suit	3 cards in 2 suits
	2 cards in 1 suit	2 cards in 1 suit

The easiest way to determine whether your hand is balanced is to remember a balanced hand cannot contain a void or a singleton. Although you may have one doubleton, you may not have more than one.

Many bids tell your partner whether the shape of your hand is balanced or unbalanced. Look closely and you will see that all balanced hands have at least two cards in every suit. Therefore, if you make a bid which promises a balanced hand, your partner knows he can count on you to have at least two cards in each of the four suits. It is good to retain this fact in your memory bank.

EXERCISE

Using a regular deck of cards, deal out four hands and determine if each of them is balanced or unbalanced. Remember, you may not have any voids or singletons in a balanced hand. You may have one doubleton but only one. After you have made the determination for each hand, keep redealing and practicing until you are confident in determining hand shapes.

OPENING THE
BIDDING

W hen you have counted your points and determined the shape of your hand, you are ready to start bidding. The conversation with your partner can begin. Your partnership is looking for an eight-card fit and trying to determine how high to go on the bidding scale.

If you make the first bid in the auction, you are said to OPEN the bidding and you are known as the OPENER. If you have the opportunity to make the first bid, how do you know if you should? When you go to a store to make a purchase, you don't go without enough money, and so it follows that you don't open the bidding without enough points. An average hand contains about 10 points, but because you are promising to take more tricks than your opponents, a better-than-average hand is needed. The bidding experts have determined a hand containing 13 total points is strong enough (don't worry about which points just concern yourself with total points).

Because we are building a solid bidding foundation, this book deals strictly with the kinds of opening hands you will encounter most often. These are hands containing 13-21 points. When you have mastered opening and responding to these hands, you will be ready to handle more unusual hands. Hands in the 13-21 point range are opened at the one level (with only one exception). If you were to open the bidding at a different level, you would be promising a different range of points. Hands, which must be opened at higher levels, are either much stronger or much weaker with unusual distribution and will be studied in advanced bidding. Remember, the goal of this book is to build a strong foundation, and taking baby steps is a very good idea.

The dealer always has the first opportunity to open the bidding. If he passes, the player to his left has the next opportunity, etc. If you have the opportunity to open the bidding, look to see if you have a hand containing 13-21 points. If you do, you are going to open the bidding at the ONE LEVEL (with only one exception). This exception is a balanced hand with 20-21 high card points which you open at the two level.

If you have 13-21 points and the opportunity to open the bidding, __OPEN THE BIDDING__ ! Players sometimes say, "I had 13 points, but I passed because they weren't very good points." For bidding purposes, one point is just as good as another. Your partner does not care which cards make up your points. He is interested in total points.

BRIDGE LANGUAGE

When you open the bidding at the one level on the bidding scale, you are saying, "I have between 13-21 points."

Without 13 total points, don't open the bidding. Simply <u>PASS</u>. But don't despair. This is a partnership game and your partner may have enough points to enter the auction. The bidding conversation begins even if you pass.

BRIDGE LANGUAGE

A pass when you have the opportunity to open the bidding says, "I do not have 13 points."

Let's say it's your turn to bid and you have counted your points. Your point range is between 13-21. You have also determined the shape of your hand (balanced or unbalanced). No one else has bid. Of course, you are going to open the bidding and open it at the one level (except for that one exception), but should you open with a bid of 1 Club, 1 Diamond, 1 Heart. 1 Spade or 1 Notrump? Each of these bids carries different information to your partner. That's how Bridge Language works. The most descriptive bid you can give your partner is an opening Notrump bid and we will discuss this opening bid first.

THE NOTRUMP OPENING BID

ALL hands fitting the following description are opened in Notrump.

1. A balanced hand
2. At least two cards in each suit.
3. For a 1 Notrump opening bid, you must have EXACTLY 15-17 HIGH CARD POINTS–do not count long cards. You may not have fewer or more high card points.
4. For a 2 Notrump opening bid, you must have exactly 20-21 HIGH CARD POINTS–do not count long cards. (This is the one exception to opening at the one level with 13-21 points.)

To open in 1 Notrump or 2 Notrump, your hand must fit these descriptions exactly. You may not have fewer or more high card points. Since you are promising a balanced hand, you may not have a void, a singleton or more than one doubleton. You are having a conversation with your partner. Give accurate information.

The Notrump opening bid is the opening bid that gives the best description of your hand. It tells your partner the shape of your hand and your point range within two or three points. It also promises at least two cards in each of the four suits. It is not often you are lucky enough to be dealt a hand fitting these Notrump descriptions, but when you are, DO NOT hesitate to open in Notrump.

BRIDGE LANGUAGE

A 1 Notrump opening bid says, "I have between 15 and 17 high card points." A 2 Notrump opening bid says, "I have 20-21 high card points." These opening bids promise a balanced hand with at least two cards in every suit.

All hands in the 13-21 point range that do not fit the description for an opening in Notrump are opened at the one level in a suit. Later, you will learn how to decide which suit to open when you can't open in a Notrump bid. For now, it is enough to know when to open 1 Notrump and when to open one-in-a-suit.

EXERCISES

Because it not necessary to know where your points are located in your hand, assume the following hands have 15-17 high card points and decide whether or not you would open 1 Notrump. Each X stands for one card in the specified suit.

	Hand 1	Hand 2	Hand 3	Hand 4
Spades	XXXX	XXXXX	XXX	XX
Hearts	XXXX	XX	XXXXX	XXX
Diamonds	XX	XXXX	XX	XXXXXXX
Clubs	XXX	XX	XXX	X

Answers: Hand 1–May be opened 1 Notrump – balanced
  Hand 2–May not be opened 1 Notrump–unbalanced
  Hand 3–May be opened 1 Notrump– balanced
  Hand 4–May not be opened 1 Notrump–unbalanced

Remember, to open 1NT, you must have between 15-17 high card points exactly. If you have 20-21 high card points and a balanced hand, open 2NT. If your balanced hand does not fit these exact HIGH CARD POINT ranges, you must open one in a suit. It is a good idea to determine your hand shape first. If your hand is balanced, look to see if your high card points fall into one of these two ranges (15-17 or 20-21). If so, do not hesitate to open in Notrump. When you are dealt such a hand, you have received a gift. Make sure you take advantage of it.

THE ONE-IN-A-SUIT OPENING BID

When a hand with a point range of 13-21 does not fulfill the requirements for opening 1 Notrump or 2 Notrump, it must be opened at the one level in a suit. The requirements for a one-in-a-suit opening bid are:

1. 13-21 points (HIGH CARD POINTS AND LONG CARD POINTS)
2. A minimum number of cards in the suit bid.
   a. Hearts and Spades <u>MUST</u> be at least <u>FIVE</u> cards in length.
   b. Clubs and Diamonds <u>MUST</u> be at least <u>THREE</u> cards in length.
3. It does not matter where your face cards are located. You are bidding according to your total point count and the number of required cards in your suits. Do not become afflicted with Face Card Hang-Up.

Remember, your goal is to find an eight card fit, and it stands to reason you must promise your partner a minimum number of cards in the suit you bid. You may have more cards than the required number, but NEVER FEWER. Does it seem strange that the length requirements are different for major and minor suits? Although you may not understand why these length requirements are required, for the time being, place your trust in the bidding experts and soon you will begin to understand. They have spent many years developing this FIVE CARD MAJOR BIDDING SYSTEM and it is the modern approach to bidding.

All suits fulfilling the length requirement qualify as opening suits. Any suit not meeting the length requirement is not eligible to be an opening suit. In case you need to be reminded, Spades and Hearts must have five or more cards and Clubs and Diamonds must have three or more cards in order to qualify. If only one suit qualifies, your decision is easy. Open the bidding in that suit. Often, however, two or more suits have enough cards to qualify. Follow these guidelines to decide which suit is the correct suit to choose:

1. If only one suit qualifies length wise, open in that suit.
2. If more than one suit qualifies lengthwise and one is longer, open in the longer suit.
3. If your eligible suits are tied in length, open in the higher-ranking suit. Recall that suits are ranked in alphabetical order – C-D-H-S.

/ 4. EXCEPTION: When the only two eligible suits are a three-card Club suit and a three-card Diamond suit, open the lower ranking Club suit (Sorry to burden you with an exception).

These guidelines help you find a fit and get to the best contract. By adhering to them, you will find there is one and only one correct suit in which to open the bidding.

BRIDGE LANGUAGE

An opening bid of 1 Heart or 1 Spade says, "I have between 13 and 21 points and at least five cards in this suit."

An opening bid of 1 Club or 1 Diamond says, "I have between 13 and 21 points and at least three cards in this suit."

Notice your only promises were your point range and a minimum number of cards in the suit you bid. You made no promises about the high card content of that suit. You will have to wait until your next bid before you are able to tell partner your hand shape and to narrow this 13-21 point range. But, for now, this is all the information you are able to give.

You have probably seen those signs that read: "Don't even think of parking here." Perhaps such a sign should also be made for Bridge: "Don't even consider opening in a suit if it does not meet its length requirement." You are looking for an eight-card fit. If you start the bidding conversation by giving your partner wrong information, how can you expect to find a fit and get to the best contract? It takes time and concentrated effort to feel confident with one-in-a-suit opening bids, but if your are beginning to see how Bridge language works, you are headed in the right direction.

Face Card Hang-Up tends to surface at this point. You are probably saying to yourself, "When I play the cards, the location of the face cards is going to be very important." This is true, but you are not playing the hand at this moment. You are beginning a bridge conversation and your job as the opener is to describe your hand according to shape, point count, and the number of cards in the suit you bid. Your focus during the auction should be on bidding. If you win the contract, you can then worry about play of the hand.

Face card strength in a particular suit has no bearing on its selection as an opening suit. Sometimes the suit you choose will have three or four face cards, and sometimes it will have one, two or none. An opening suit is chosen strictly by its length and rank, not by face card content. In fact, there are absolutely no high-card requirements for any of the suits. Do not allow Face Card Hang-Up to interfere with your decision.

REVIEW

It is important to understand each step in the bidding system before you proceed. You are trying to build a strong foundation and should not go forward until you are confident with each step. Do yourself a favor and before you proceed, make sure you know:

1. How to count your points correctly.
2. How to determine if your hand is balanced or unbalanced.
3. That hands in the 13-21 point range are opened at the one level on the bidding scale except for balanced hands with 20-21 high card points which are opened 2 Notrump.
4. The qualifications for a 1 Notrump opening bid are 15-17 high card points (no fewer and no more) and a balanced hand. Balanced hands with 20-21 high card points (no fewer and no more) are opened 2NT.
5. If your hand does not qualify for an opening Notrump bid, you must open one in a suit. This bid is not nearly as descriptive, but you will describe your hand further with your second bid.
6. Hearts and Spades must be at least five cards in length to qualify as opening suits. These suits may be longer but not shorter.
7. Clubs and Diamonds must be at least three cards in length to be considered as opening suits. These suits may be longer but not shorter.
8. How to select the correct suit to open if more than one suit meets the length requirement.

When you feel secure in all of the above, proceed. If you do not feel secure, go back and review.

SUGGESTED EXERCISES

Take a regular deck of cards and deal out four hands. Although there is only one opener for each hand, pretend that each hand would have the opportunity to open the bidding. First decide the shape of each hand (balanced or unbalanced). Then decide which hands have enough strength (13-21 points). If a hand does not have the required strength, pass. If it is balanced, determine if it has the correct number of high card points to be opened with a Notrump bid. If it cannot be opened in Notrump, decide in which suit to open at the one level. Repeat this exercise until you feel comfortable. It is good to do this exercise with another player so you can discuss the hands.

OPENERS AND RESPONDERS

The two players in a partnership take on different responsibilities according to who they are in the bidding auction. If you make the first bid in the auction, you are the OPENER because you begin or start the auction. Once you have opened the bidding you have a job to do. With each bid, you must describe your hand to the best of your ability. Your goal until a fit is found is to tell your partner whether your hand is balanced or unbalanced and your point range. You are the information giver and this remains your job throughout the auction.

If your partner opens the bidding, you respond to his bid and are known as the RESPONDER. As responder, you gather information from the opener and add it to what is in your hand and try to steer your partnership to the best contract. You are the CAPTAIN of the partnership. Your responsibility is to try to find an eight-card fit with your partner and determine how high your partnership should bid on the bidding scale. Unlike the opener, it is not your job to always describe your hand. Many times you (the responder) will withhold information until more is known about the opener's hand. Can you see the difference in responsibilities for the opener and responder?

1. The opener tries to give the responder the best possible description of his hand. (point range, balanced or unbalanced, number of cards in the suits he bids). This is how you find a fit and also help responder decide how high to go on the bidding scale.
2. The opener states facts about his hand.
3. The responder gives the opener some information, but, mostly, he asks for information until a final contract can be reached.
4. The responder tries to decide if the hand should be played with a particular suit as trump or in a Notrump contract, and how high to bid.
5. If you can remember who you are in the auction and what your responsibilities are, your success will skyrocket.

You are not expected to know how to do this just yet, for now, concentrate on the responsibilities of the opener and the responder. You will learn how the opener and responder go about carrying out these duties as we progress.

SCORING AND CONTRACTS

Y ou are now prepared to begin bidding, but before you start, you should have some idea about how hands are scored. When you open the bidding, you are saying you can take more tricks than your opponents. Therefore, you are saying you can take more than six tricks. If you win the bidding auction and make enough tricks to fulfill your contract, you score trick points for all tricks taken over six (these six tricks are called BOOK). What each trick over book is worth depends on whether the contract is in Clubs, Diamonds, Hearts, Spades or Notrump.

TRICK POINTS FOR THE DIFFERENT CONTRACTS

Clubs.......................................20 points
Diamonds...............................20 points
Hearts.....................................30 points

Spades.......................................30 points

Noturmp............................. 40 for the first trick

30 for each additional

Trick

For example, if you bid 3 Spades and make nine tricks (book + 3 = 9), you have made your contract and score 90 trick points. You are awarded 90 points because in a Spade contract each trick taken over six (book) is worth 30 trick points. A contract of 3 Clubs scores 60 points because the trick points given for Clubs is 20 points for each trick over book. A contract of 2 Notrump scores 70 points because you are awarded 40 for the first trick and 30 for the second.

Any contract scoring fewer than 100 trick points is called a **PART SCORE CONTRACT.** Contracts scoring at least 100 points are called **GAME CONTRACTS.** The number of tricks you need to take to score 100 points depends on whether your contract is in Clubs, Diamonds, Hearts, Spades or Notrump. Game contracts are very attractive because not only are trick points scored, but a large bonus is awarded when you bid and make a contract scoring 100 points.

If you do not bid a game contract, you cannot score bonus points even if you take enough tricks to score 100 points. For example, if you bid 4 Spades and take 10 tricks, you score 120 trick points and are awarded a large bonus. If you bid 3 Spades and make 10 tricks, you score 120 trick points, ninety for the tricks you bid over book and thirty for the overtrick. However, you are not awarded bonus points because you didn't bid a game contract. Because of the very attractive bonus, you hope your partnership's combined point count (the points you counted when you valued your hands) is enough to bid a contract that scores at least 100 trick points. It is your goal to make sure you reach a game contract if your partnership has enough points.

If you bid and make 12 or 13 tricks, these are called **SLAM CONTRACTS** and they carry even larger bonus points. This book teaches how to get to a part score or game contract, but does not venture into slam bidding. Bidding a slam contract requires advanced bidding techniques and it is recommended you postpone this until you are secure in basic bidding procedures. Trying to learn too much too quickly usually backfires.

EXERCISES

1. What are trick points?
   Answer: Points given for all tricks taken over book (6) if you make your contract.

2. How many trick points are given for:

STRAIN	ANSWER
a. Club	20 points
b. Diamonds	20 points
c. Hearts	30 points
d. Spades	30 points
e. Notrump	40 points for 1st trick
	30 for all other tricks

3. What is a game contract?
   Answer: A contract scoring 100 or more trick points

4. What is a part score contract?
   Answer: A contract scoring fewer than 100 trick points

5. Why do you want to reach a game contract?
   Answer: If you make it, you receive a large bonus!

6. If you don't bid a game contract but take enough tricks to score 100 or more trick points, are you awarded the game bonus?
   Answer: No, you must both bid and make a game contract to receive the bonus.

To have a good chance of making a particular game contract, the bidding experts recommend your partnership have a minimum number of combined points. During the bidding process, the opener tells the responder his point count, to which responder adds his own count. The combined total determines how high the partnership should go on the bidding scale. You are always hoping to find enough points to bid a game contract. Use the table below to determine how many points are needed for a particular game contract.

POINTS NEEDED TO BID A GAME CONTRACT

GAME	TRICK SCORE	TRICKS	POINTS
3 Notrump	100	9	25
4 Spades	120	10	25
4 Hearts	120	10	25
5 Diamonds	100	11	29
5 Clubs	100	11	29

Don't panic. You will soon learn how to determine the combined point count of your hands. For now, just be aware of how many combined points are needed to bid a game contract in Clubs, Diamonds, Hearts, Spades or Notump. Do you see the need for an accurate point count? Many game contracts are missed because one or both members of a partnership didn't count correctly.

THE SOUGHT AFTER GAME CONTRACTS

The 3 Notrump, 4 Heart and 4 Spade contracts are desirable because they require fewer points and fewer tricks must be taken. At first glance, it may seem as though 3 Notrump would be the most desirable of all game contracts. After all, only nine tricks need to be taken. This may surprise you, but even though you must take one more trick, a major suit contract is superior because you have a trump suit to help you and a trump suit is a powerful tool. With the same number of points, you will usually score at least one more trick with a trump suit and the hand is easier to play. As the name says, a

Notrump contract is played without a trump suit. The game contracts of 4 Hearts and 4 Spades are the most sought after contracts.

The game contracts requiring 25 combined points are the ones you are interested in bidding. If your partnership has 25 combined points, you could play in 3 Notrump, 4 Hearts or 4 Spades. However, always prefer to play your game contract in a major suit game contract. Therefore, when you bid, top priority is given to finding an eight-card fit in a major suit.

GAME CONTRACTS YOU ARE RELUCTANT TO BID

The minor suit contracts, 5 Clubs and 5 Diamonds, are the least desirable of all the game contracts because 29 combined points are required and 11 tricks must be taken. These contracts are much more difficult to bid and make.

When you and your partner have exchanged enough information and know you have 25 points but your only eight-card fit is in a minor suit, you could continue to bid in hopes of finding the extra four points needed to bid 5 Clubs or 5 Diamonds. If you continue, you often find yourself at the four level in the minor suit and then realize you do not have 29 points to bid to the five level. A four-level minor suit contract scores only 80 trick points and doesn't award game bonus points. Once you have bid to the four level, you have gone past 3 Notrump on the bidding scale. A 4 Notrump contract scores 130 points, but because there is no trump suit, it is even more difficult to make than 5 Clubs or 5 Diamonds. Besides, the 4 Notrump bid is rarely used in a routine auction. It is a special bid used when there is a possibility of a slam contract.

An explanation of that special bid is not given in this book, but know that the 4 Notrump bid has a special purpose and is generally used in advanced bidding. By continuing to bid beyond 3 Notrump, you run the risk of missing a game contract and the bonus points that go with it. If you have found 25 points and the only fit you have found is in a minor suit, the bidding experts recommend bidding a 3 Notrump game contract. This probably sounds like a contradiction, because you must play the hand without the benefit of a trump suit, but it is better than pursuing a 5 Club or 5 Diamond contract. Although your minor suit fit won't give the hand as much power as it would as a trump suit, it is still very helpful when the hand is played in a Notrump contract.

Neither the five-level minor suit contract nor the 3 Notrump contract will work every time you bid them, but experience has shown that 99 times out or 100, the 3 Notrump contract is the best choice. Those odds may not be exact, but they are close enough. With 25 points and only a minor suit fit, you will have more success if you choose to play the game contract of 3 Notrump. For those who have played before, understand this is the modern approach and a much better way of bidding.

Even if you can't find an eight card fit, a game contract should be bid if you have 25 combined points. Without a trump suit or an eight-card fit, a game contract is more difficult to make and involves a certain amount of risk, but the possible bonus points make the risk worthwhile. The best choice in this situation is also 3 Notrump.

Bridge parallels life. There are no guarantees even if you do everything right. You may not be able to fulfill a game contract even if you have an eight-card major suit trump fit and 25 points. Many variables affect the outcome of a hand, including just plain luck, but if you have the opportunity to bid a game contract, take it.

WHAT IF WE DON'T HAVE ENOUGH POINTS FOR A GAME CONTRACT?

As soon as you discover your partnership does not have the 25 points needed to bid a game contract, stop bidding at a low level. If you can't bid a game contract, why bid any higher than necessary? You run the risk of GOING DOWN, or failing to make your contract and allowing the defenders to score penalty points. Even though part score contracts are not awarded large bonuses, you score trick points for fulfilling your contract and trick points are also given for all OVERTRICKS (tricks made in excess of your contract).

If you have determined the hand must be played in a part-score contract, bid low and in a suit if you have a fit. A trump suit is particularly helpful when you are lacking in points. For example, if you know there is a fit in Diamonds, bid a 2 Diamond contract rather than staying in 1 Notrump. This may be confusing because 1 Notrump is lower on the bidding scale than 2 Diamonds. Actually, because of the power the trump suit adds, 2 Diamonds is easier to make because you have a trump suit. With the same number of points, you usually make at least one more trick with a trump suit and it is much easier to play. If this sounds confusing, don't worry, you will learn more about this as you progress.

REVIEW

1. You need 13-21 points to open the auction at the one level. Unbalanced hands within this point range are ALWAYS opened at the ONE level and are opened one-in-a-suit. Count high card points and long card points and follow the length and rank guidelines to select the correct suit in which to open.

2. With 15-17 high card points and a balanced hand, open 1 Notrump. With 20-21 high card points and a balanced hand, open 2 Notrump. Your hand must be balanced and in these exact high card point ranges.

3. With 13-21 points and a balanced hand that does not fit the descriptions for opening in 1 Notrump or 2 Notrump is opened one-in-a-suit. Follow the length and rank guidelines to select the correct suit to bid.

4. If you make your contract, trick points are given for all tricks taken over six (book). The number of points given per trick depends on whether your

contract is in Clubs, Diamonds, Hearts, Spades or Notrump. These are called strains.

5. Any contract scoring 100 trick points when bid and made is called a game contract.

6. Game contracts are sought after because large bonus points are awarded for bidding and making them.

7. Top priority in bidding is given to finding an eight-card Heart or Spade fit (major suit fit). With 25 combined points, you want to play the game in a major suit contract, if possible.

8. With 25 points and the only fit to be found is a minor suit fit, bid 3 Notrump. You are not interested in pursuing a 5 Club or 5 Diamond contract.

9. With 25 points and no fit to be found, bid 3 Notrump.

10. Without 25 points, stop bidding at a low level and play in a trump fit (major or minor suit)if possible (more on this later).

EXERCISES

1. How many points must you score for game contracts?
Answer: At least 100 points.

2. Must you both bid and make a game contract to receive the bonus?
Answer: Yes, you must both bid and make a game contract to receive the bonus. If you do not bid a game contract, you will not receive the bonus even if you take enough tricks to score 100 points.

3. What are the three most desirable game contracts? Why?
   Answer: 4 Hearts, 4 Spades, 3 Notrump–they require 25 points and require fewer tricks to be taken.

4. Of these three game contracts, which are the most sought after?
   Answer: The major suit games of 4 Hearts and 4 Spades.

5. What contract do you usually bid if you have an eight-card fit is in a minor suit and you have 25 points?
   Answer: 3 Notrump

6. With 25 points, should you bid game even without a fit? If so, what game?
   Answer: Yes, 3 Notrump.

7. If you discover game is out of reach (your partnership has less than 25 points), What do you do?
   Answer: Stop bidding at a low level and in a trump fit if possible–It makes no difference whether it is a major or minor suit fit as you are playing for a part score.

FEAR AND BIDDING

Before the bidding auctions, let's discuss a common problem among new players. Many are afraid to bid because they don't know how to play the hand very well. Failing to make your bid can be embarrassing. Players would rather not bid to a high level to make sure their contracts can be fulfilled when the hand is played. The opportunity to earn game bonus points is often missed because a player fears embarrassment.

Try to separate the two stages of the game. Even though you don't know much about the play of the hand, learn to bid it correctly. Keep in mind you are not always going to play the hand. For example, if partner bids the final strain first, he will be playing the hand. That lets you off the hook about 50% of the time. Partner will appreciate you more if you bid according to the number of points in your hand, not the confidence in your playing ability. Have faith. Your playing ability will improve with more playing experience. You may not make your bid often at first, but that should not prevent you from being in the correct contract.

TEAMWORK AND GETTING RID OF GREED

Because the bidding auction is an information exchange, think of it as a conversation. In order to have a good conversation, it is necessary to give accurate information and be willing to listen to what your partner has to say. The importance of communication and cooperation cannot be stressed too strongly or often enough. TEAMWORK, TEAMWORK, TEAMWORK! The element of GREED should not be a part of your bidding behavior. There will be times when you are dealt a strong, beautiful hand. You may even fall in love with it. Because you were the lucky one dealt this wonderful hand, you may feel entitled to name the trump suit and play the hand. This may come as a shock, but just because you hold the stronger hand doesn't automatically entitle you to be the declarer. That may or may not be what is best for your partnership. Although it is sometimes difficult to accept the role of dummy, think of your partnership as a team. Both hands of the partnership must be taken into consideration before a decision is made and that is done in an honest, unselfish bidding conversation.

The auction is not the time to compete against your partner, but to cooperate and communicate for the sake of the partnership. Remember who you are in the auction (opener or responder) and carry out your responsibilities. Every Bridge player dreams of having an unselfish partner. Do your best to make your partner's dreams come true.

Now, you have counted your points, decided your hand shape and know what you are looking for in the auction. In case you need to be reminded, you are looking for an eight-card (any cards) fit, enough points for a game contract and, if possible, a major suit game contract.

The bidding conversation begins with the opening bid. If your partner has opened 1 Notrump, he has 15-17 high card points. If he opened 2 Notrump, he has 20-21 high card points. If he opened one-in-a-suit, he has 13-21 total points. Because of the differences in the point ranges, the responses to these opening bids are not the same. We are going to consider the responses to the opening one-in-a-suit bid first.

RESPONDING TO A ONE-IN-A-SUIT OPENING BID

The majority of hands are opened at the one level in a suit. This opening bid is not very descriptive. It promises at least 13 points, but there could be as many as 21. An opening bid of 1 Heart or 1 Spade guarantees at least five cards in the suit bid and an opening bid of 1 Club or 1 Diamond guarantees at least three cards in the suit bid. That is all the information the opener gives with a one-in-a-suit opening bid. Absolutely nothing is known about the strength of the suit he bid, his other suits or the shape of his hand. The responder can not set the contract until he gets more information.

WHEN PARTNER OPENS ONE-IN-A-SUIT, AND YOU HAVE 0-5 POINTS, YOU MUST <u>PASS</u>. WITH 6 OR MORE POINTS, YOU MUST RESPOND.

You are gathering information in an effort to find an eight-card fit and trying to decide how high to bid on the bidding scale. Because the major suit game contracts are the most desirable, top priority is given to finding a major suit fit.

Ok, it is time to learn how to respond to partner's opening bid of one-in-a- suit. Your answer will depend on whether or not you have found a major suit fit and the number of points you hold.

If your partner opened in a major suit, your partnership may already have found a major suit fit. He promised five cards in his suit. Do you have three? If you have three or more cards (any cards) in his suit, the search for a major suit fit is over. You do not need to look for a better fit. Even if you have the other major suit and it is a very good one, the search is over.

RESPONDING TO A ONE-LEVEL MAJOR SUIT OPENING BID WHEN YOU HAVE THREE OR MORE CARDS IN OPENER'S MAJOR SUIT

When your partner opens in a major suit and you have at least three cards in his suit, you are one lucky Bridge player. Your goal of finding a major suit fit has been accomplished before you make your first response. Watch out for Face Card Hang-Up. The three cards you hold in his suit may be the Ace, King and Queen or they may be the two, three and four. It makes no difference. The only requirement for a strong trump fit is at least eight cards and they may be any cards.

Sometimes, you have three cards in your partner's major suit, and you also have a strong suit of your own. Being only human, you'll probably have a burning desire to tell your partner about your wonderful suit. Resist greed. Even if your suit is loaded with face cards, be satisfied with one major suit fit. Your strong suit will be just as valuable after all the trumps have been drawn.

Once a major suit fit has been found and your partnership wins the contract, the contract is played in that fit. The only determination left is how high the partnership should bid, which depends on your partnership's combined point count. An accurate point count must be done and the value of your hand may have increased because a major suit fit has been found. Points are added for any and all voids, singletons, and doubletons in the dummy hand. These are distribution points called **DUMMY POINTS** and are **ONLY** added when you have found a **MAJOR SUIT FIT** and **YOUR** hand will be the dummy hand.

DUMMY POINTS

      Void..................................5 points
      Singleton............................3 points
      Doubleton...........................1 point

THE LOWDOWN ON DUMMY POINTS

Think this out logically. You have found a major suit fit. If your partnership wins the contract, this major suit will be the trump suit. Because your partner mentioned the suit first, he is the declarer and you are the dummy.

The cards you hold in your partner's suit become trump cards in the dummy hand. If the dummy hand has any voids, singletons or doubletons, dummy's trumps can be used to take tricks in those short suits. For example: If the dummy is void in the suit led, a trump from dummy can be used to immediately win the trick. If the dummy has a singleton, a trump can be used the second time the suit is played. A doubleton isn't quite as useful because you can't trump until the third round but it must be given some value. When declarer uses a trump in DUMMY to take a trick in another suit, he takes a trick he would not take otherwise.

You originally valued your hand giving point value to high cards and long cards. Now you know you have a trump suit and declarer can take tricks in your short suits with your trump cards in the dummy. If you have dummy points to add, DO NOT give point value to your long cards because you probably won't be using them to take tricks. It would be nice to count it all, but your hand would be overvalued.

Dummy points are added because the declarer can use dummy's trumps to take tricks in dummy's short suits. Without a trump suit, voids, singletons and doubletons have no added value. In fact, they may prove to be a liability rather than an asset. With 25 points and a minor suit fit, the hand is almost always played in Notrump. There is no trump suit in a Notrump contract, and it follows that no dummy points are given for minor suit fits.

EXERCISES

1. What are dummy points and who adds them?
   Answer: These are distribution points added when a player finds a fit with his partner's MAJOR suit. They are ONLY added by the player who will be the DUMMY. The player who mentions the suit first, will be the declarer and does not add dummy points as his hand will not be the dummy when the hand is played.

2. Why are dummy points added?
   Answer: They are added because declarer will be able to use dummy's trumps to take tricks in dummy's short suits (void, singleton, or doubleton suits). These are tricks he would not take otherwise.

3. If you are going to add dummy points, do you give value to your long cards?
   Answer: No, to do so would overvalue your hand.

4. What is the dummy point value of a void, singleton, or doubleton?
   Answer: 5 for a void, 3 for a singleton, 1 for a doubleton.

PARTNER OPENED IN A MAJOR SUIT AND YOU HAVE THREE CARDS IN HIS SUIT

You have a major suit fit. Add your points including dummy points. All that is left to decide is how high your partnership should bid.

0-5 points..........PASS.
6-9 points..........Raise his suit to 2 Level.
(SINGLE RAISE)
10-11 points......Jump to the three level in his suit.
(LIMIT RAISE)
12+ points.........Bid a new suit.

BRIDGE LANGUAGE

A pass in response to one in a suit opening bid says, "Partner, I can't help you. I don't even have six points."

A single raise of the opener's suit says, "We have a fit in your suit. My point range is 6-9. Add this to your point count and pass or bid on if you see game as a possibility."

A jump in partner's opening suit says, "We have a fit in your suit and I have 10-11 points. Add this to your point count and pass or bid game if you can count 25 total points."

The bid of a new suit by the responder says, "I have four cards in this new suit and need more information."

When you raise your partner's suit, you are saying you have a fit and communicating your point count. You are allowing him to decide if a game level contract is possible. All he needs to do is add his points to those promised with your raise. He may pass if he sees no possibility of a game contract, invite you to bid game if he thinks it may be possible or bid game himself if he knows your partnership has enough combined points.

With 12 points and a major suit fit, you are definitely going to play the contract in your partner's major suit and you know there are enough points for a game contract (12 + 13 = 25). You should have no intention of letting the auction die until at least a game level contract in opener's major suit has been reached. Although a direct jump to game in his suit would seem the logical bid, maybe a game contract isn't high enough. Remember, your partner could have as many as 21 points. Perhaps you have enough combined points to bid a slam. SMALL SLAMS (six level bids) require 33 points and GRAND SLAMS (seven level bids) require 37 points. A final decision can't be made until you know more about your partner's point range and he will tell you that with his next bid.

If you jump to game level in his suit, he will pass and the auction will be over. But, you don't want the auction to end before you have the information you need. The way to get that information is to bid a new suit. There is no need to worry that partner will pass because ALL NEW SUITS BID BY THE RESPONDER ARE FORCING. He is forced to make another bid. (This is an example of the responder withholding information in an effort to learn more about the opener's hand.) All new suits by the responder promise at least four cards in that suit (regardless of the suit bid).

Partner's next bid will tell you his point range within three points. After you hear his second bid, you can determine if slam is out of the question.

Although techniques for slam bidding are not addressed in this book, you should learn how to prepare for such bidding. For now, be satisfied with a game level contract, but take the long way around – make a forcing bid of a new suit first and then bid game in partner's major on your second bid.

EXERCISES

1. With a regular deck of cards, shuffle and deal four hands. Assume all four hands are responding to a 1 Heart opening bid. Decide if there is a fit–remember, that an opening bid in a major suit promises five cards in that suit. If any of the hands have a fit, count your points including dummy points and decide how you would respond. Repeat this exercise until you feel confident.
2. Do the same exercise but this time assume you are responding to a 1 Spade opening bid. What is your point count and response?

These exercises may seem repetitive, but players are always forgetting to add dummy points. You cannot reach the correct level on the bidding scale if you neglect to count all your points.

RESPONDING TO AN OPENING BID OF ONE IN A SUIT WHEN YOU DO NOT HAVE A MAJOR SUIT FIT

This time you weren't so lucky. Either your partner opened in a major suit for which you do not have three-card support or he opened in a minor suit. If he opened in a minor suit and you have five cards in support of his suit, you have a minor suit fit. However, finding a major suit fit is still your top priority. Simply place this minor suit fit on the back burner while you search for a major suit fit (another example of responder withholding information until he knows more about the opener's hand.)

You are hoping to locate a major suit fit, but more information is needed. The way to get more information is to bid a new suit. Remember how the bid of a new suit by the responder says, "I need more information." It actually accomplishes two objectives. It suggests another suit as a possible fit and forces the opener to bid again. Opener's second bid will tell you more about his hand.

Just as opening suits must meet certain length requirements, the suits bid by the responder must also meet a length requirement. In fact, after the opening bid, any bid of a new suit by either the opener or the responder promises FOUR cards (you could have more). This requirement is the same for all suits (Clubs, Diamonds,

Hearts and Spades). With more than one suit of four or more cards, use these guidelines to select the correct one:

a. Bid the longest first if your hand is strong enough. (more on this later).
b. With two five card or longer suits tied in length, bid the higher ranking first.
c. If all suits are four card suits, bid them up the rank line. (Clubs, Diamonds, Hearts, Spades).

Always bid the new suit you choose at the lowest level possible. Even if you have a very strong hand, there is no need to show that strength with your first bid. As the responder, you are gathering information to determine the best contract. Bidding your new suit at the lowest possible level keeps the bidding under control until you can make that determination. You get the information you need without wasting valuable space on the bidding scale. Don't worry that partner will pass. A NEW SUIT BY RESPONDER IS FORCING. OPENER MUST BID AGAIN.

Here again, Face Card Hang-Up may rear its ugly head. Face card strength in the new suit is unimportant. You are promising your partner a minimum number of cards (four), not strength. Those cards may be the Ace, King, Queen or Jack or they may be the two, three, four and five. It makes no difference. Follow the guidelines and do not be influenced by face cards.

Without a major suit fit, the bid of a new suit is always the bid you would like to make. However, there are three times when you cannot or should not bid a new suit:

1. You do not have a new suit of four or more cards.
2. Your point range is 6-9 and your only four card or longer suit must be bid at the two level. With this point range, you cannot bid a new suit at the two level.
3. With a balanced hand and 13 or more HIGH CARD POINTS, the bid of a new suit is the bid you would like to make. However, with this hand shape and point count, there is a restriction. You may bid any new suit of four or more cards at the one level, but a five card suit is needed if you must take the bidding to the two level. (explanations and what to do to follow)

With only 6-9 points, it is not a good idea to push your partner up the bidding scale until you know more about the strength of his hand. For that reason, the bidding experts have found at least 10 points are needed for responder to bid a new suit at the two level. If your partner opens 1 Spade, you need at least 10 points to bid 2 Clubs, 2 Diamonds or 2 Hearts. If he opens 1 Diamond, you may bid 1 Heart or 1 Spade, but you need at least 10 points to bid 2 Clubs. Even if you have a very long suit, you need at least 10 points to bid it at the two level. Simply ignore all new suits that must be bid at the two level if your hand is in the 6-9 point range. If partner opened in a minor suit and you have five cards (occasionally four cards) in his suit and no suit you can bid at the one level, raise partner's minor suit to the two level. If you can't do that, bid 1 Notrump. This 1 Notrump bid is a bid of last resort and does not promise a balanced hand. The only promise it makes is six points. You are simply keeping the bidding open for partner who could have as many as 21 points.

With a balanced hand of 13 or more HIGH CARD POINTS, a new suit is your best bid but there is a restriction. With this hand shape and point count, you may bid a suit of four or more cards at the one level. However, to bid a new suit at the two level, it must be a five card suit. Without either of these, you may not bid a new suit. If you are unable to bid a new suit, jump to 2 Notrump with 13-15 high card points. This bid promises a balanced hand and is forcing. Jump to 3 Notrump with 16-18 high card points. If you jump to 3 Notrump, you are already at game level and it is not a forcing bid. Opener may pass 3 Notrump or bid again according to what his hand holds. There is a very good reason the bidding experts require this restriction but it is complicated. For now, know following this rule will lead you to the correct bid.

RESPONSES TO ONE-IN-A-SUIT OPENING BID WHEN A MAJOR SUIT FIT HAS NOT BEEN FOUND AND YOU HAVE 6-11 POINTS

1. The bid of a new suit is your first choice.
2. Without a new suit that can be bid:
   A. If your partner opened in a minor suit and you have five card support, you have a minor suit fit. (occasionally, you support with four cards)

    a.   6-9 points, raise your partner's minor suit to the two level. This is a SINGLE RAISE.

    b.   With 10-11 points and a minor suit fit, raise your partner's minor suit to the three level. This is a LIMIT RAISE.

B. With 6-9 points and no new suit to bid at the one level and no minor suit fit, there is only one option. Bid 1 Notrump (this only promises 6-9 points and says nothing about the shape of your hand). It is just a way to keep the auction open for partner who could have as many as 21 points. Think of it as a bid of last resort. It is not a forcing bid.

BRIDGE LANGUAGE

When the responder raises the opener's minor suit to the two level, it says, "My point range is 6-9 and we have a fit in your suit. I have no new suit I can bid at the one level. Pass or bid on if you see game as a possibility."

When the responder raises the opener's minor suit to the three level, it says, "My point range is 10-11 and we have a fit. I have no new suit to bid. Pass or bid on if you see game as a possibility."

In Bridge language, the same bid can have very different meanings depending on the stage of the auction. For example, the 1 Notrump bid by the opener promises 15-17 high card points, a balanced hand and at least two cards in each suit. A 1 Notrump response by the responder promises only 6-9 points. It says nothing about the shape of his hand (balanced or unbalanced) or the un-bid suits. It is just a way for responder to keep the bidding open for partner who could have as many as 21 points and is not a forcing bid. The bidding experts have built safeguards into the system to keep the bidding from getting out of control without enough points. A 1 Notrump bid by the responder is one of those safeguards.

BRIDGE LANGUAGE

When the responder bids 1 Notrump in response to partner's opening bid, he is saying, "I do not have a suit I can bid at the one level or a fit with your suit but I have 6-9 points. I bid 1 Notrump to keep the bidding open for you. This is not a forcing bid"

WITH 12 OR MORE POINTS: RESPONSES TO A ONE-IN-A-SUIT OPENING BID WITHOUT A MAJOR SUIT FIT

1. With an UNBALANCED hand:
   a. The bid of a new suit is your first choice. With this point count, bid a major suit at the ONE level if you can. Otherwise, bid as usual–longest first, higher ranking of two five card or longer suits tied in length or up the line with four card suits.
   b. If you have no new suit you can bid, you must have a fit for partner's minor suit. In that case, jump to game in your partner's minor suit (3 Notrump).

2. With a BALANCED hand and 13+ HIGH CARD POINTS:

a. Your first preference in response to an opening one-in-a-suit bid is a new suit. However, with this hand shape and point count, you may bid any four card or longer suit at the one level, but to bid a new suit at the two level, a five card suit is required. If you can't do either, jump to 2 Notrump with 13-15 high card points or 3 Notrump with 16-18 high card points. The jump to 2 Notrump is forcing. The opener must bid again. Opener may pass 3 Notrump or bid on according to what he holds in his hand.

BRIDGE LANGUAGE

In response to a one-in-a-suit opening bid, a jump to 2 Notrump says, "I do not have a four card or longer suit I can bid at the one level or a five card suit I can bid at the two level, but I have a balanced hand with 13-15 high card points. This jump to 2 Notrump is forcing. A jump to 3 No-trump promises balanced hand with 16-18 high card points."

That was a lot to absorb wasn't it? All novice players have difficulty with the responder's first bid. But it's not as difficult as it seems. If your partner opened in a major suit and you have three card support, you have found your major suit fit. The search is over. All you need to determine is how high to bid, and that is just a matter of adding points. If you have not found a major suit fit, you need more information. If you can bid a new suit, it is always the bid you would like to make. Usually, this is possible but there are the three restrictions. Study these and you will know when this is not possible and what to bid otherwise.

REVIEW
RESPONDING TO A ONE-IN-A-SUIT OPENING BID

1. You are looking for an eight-card fit. Give priority to finding a major suit fit.
2. If your partner opened in a major suit and you have three-card support, the hand is played in that suit if you win the contract. Respond in his suit according to your point range including dummy points.
3. Without a major suit fit, you must bid with SIX or more points. Pass with 0-5 points.
4. To respond in a new suit at the two level, you must have 10 points. With only 6-9 points, ignore all suits that must be bid at the two level. If you can't bid a new suit or support your partner's minor suit, bid 1 Notrump. This is not a forcing bid and makes no promises other than 6-9 points.
5. Responder's jump to 2 Notrump shows a balanced hand with 13-15 high card points, no new suit to bid at the one level and no five card suit to bid at the two level. This bid is forcing.
6. Responder's jump to 3 Notrump shows a balanced hand and 16-18 high card points and is not forcing.

EXERCISES

1. Your partner opened 1 Heart or 1 Spade, how many cards do you need in his suit to have a fit?
Answer: Three——he promised 5 with his opening bid.

2. What should you do when you discover you have a major suit fit?
Answer: Look to see if you have any short suits and, if so, re-evaluate your point count with dummy points if you can–5 for void, 3 for singleton, and 1 for a doubleton.

3. Do you give value to long cards if you are adding dummy points?
Answer: No, to do so would overvalue your hand.

4. Your partner opened 1 Heart or 1 Spade and you have a fit, What do you respond with:

Responder's
point count   Answers
0-5 points..........PASS
6-9 points..........Raise his suit to the two level.
10-11 points.......Jump to three level in his suit
12+ points..........Bid a new suit for more information.

5. Your partner opened 1 Diamond or 1 Club. If you have 5 cards in his suit, you have a minor suit fit. Do you immediately raise his suit?

Answer: No, your first priority is to find a major suit fit. Do you have a new suit of four or more cards? If so, bid it if you have enough points.

6. Make sure you know how to choose which new suit to bid.

EXERCISES

Deal four hands with a regular deck. Add your points. With each hand, ask yourself what you would respond if your partner opened 1 Club, 1 Diamond, 1 Heart or 1 Spade. Keeping the last chapter handy, decide with each hand what you would respond if partner opened 1Club then 1Diamond then 1Heart and finally 1Spade. If you are in doubt, check back to this chapter to help you. It is very beneficial to do this exercise with a partner. In that way, you can check on each other. Keep dealing and responding as above until you feel comfortable with responding to one-in-a-suit opening bid. Be sure to check for dummy points with major suit fit.

After you have finished , use the following checklist to decide if it is time to move ahead. If you are not comfortable with anything on this list, do not proceed. Instead, practice what causes you trouble. You should now know:

1. How to give your hand point value.
2. How to determine your hand shape.

3. How to decide if your hand fits the description to open 1 Notrump or 2 Notrump.

4. How to decide if your hand should be opened at the one level in a suit, and if so, how to choose the correct suit in which to open.

5. How to count dummy points and when to add them.

6. How to respond with a major suit fit with 6-9 points, 10-11 points, and 12 or more. Include dummy points.

7. Why you bid a new suit when you have a major suit fit and 12 or more points even though you are sure of 25 (enough for a game contract).

8. When you have not found a major suit fit, your top priority is to search for one. Offer another four card or longer suit as a possible fit. The bid of a new suit also asks for more information about your partner's hand. All new suits (Clubs, Diamonds, Hearts and Spades) bid after the opening bid by either the opener or the responder promise 4 cards. They could have more cards but not fewer.

9. If you have a fit for partner's minor suit and don't have a new suit you can bid (you don't have one or don't have 10 points to bid the one you have at the two level) raise your partner's minor with five (occasionally four) card support. Raise his suit to the two level with 6-9 points. Raise to three level with 10-11 points.

10. With 6-9 points and no suit to bid at the one level and no four or five-card minor suit support, your

only option to keep the bidding open for partner is 1 Notrump. You must say something as partner could have as many as 21. This is a last resort response and the only promise it makes is six points.

11. When you have a balanced hand with 13-15 high card points, bid a new four card or longer suit at the one level or five card suit at the two level. If you can't do either, make a forcing bid by jumping to 2 Notrump. With 16-18 high card points and a balanced hand, jump to 3 Notrump.

12. With 12 points and no fit for partner, bid a major suit at the one level if you can. If not, bid as usual– Longest suit first, higher ranking of two five card or longer suits tied in length, bid four card suits up the rank line Clubs-Diamonds-Hearts-Spades.

OPENER'S REBID

Recall your responsibility as the opener. It is to describe your hand to your partner. He wants to know whether your hand is balanced or unbalanced and wants you to narrow your original 13-21 point range. If a fit has been found (major or minor suit fit), there is no need to continue looking. All you need to communicate is your point range. If you have not found a fit, your second bid (or rebid, as it is called) will give him a much clearer picture of your hand. Be fore-warned, the bidding can become tedious at this stage and requires some concentrated effort. If you feel confident in what you have learned so far, hang in there.

Again, determine your hand shape (balanced or unbalanced), then count your points (accurately) and place the count in one of these three ranges:

        13-15...................minimum hand
        16-18...................medium hand
        19-21...................maximum hand

You are actually dividing the 13-21 point range you originally promised into three smaller ranges of three points each. To help you remember, say to yourself, " I started with 13 so the small range must be 13-15, the medium range must be 16-18 and the maximum range must be 19-21."

If a fit has been found (a major suit fit or a minor suit fit), all you need to communicate is in which of these three ranges your point range belongs. If a fit has not been found, you must try to communicate both the shape of your hand and in which of the smaller point ranges your hand belongs.

OPENER'S REBID WHEN A FIT HAS BEEN FOUND

Have you found a fit? If your partner raised your suit or you have four cards in the suit he bid, the answer is "yes". The search is over regardless of whether the fit is in a major or a minor suit. At this stage, there is no need to search for a better fit. All that is left to determine is how high to bid (game or part score).

Help your partner determine how high your partnership should go on the bidding scale by showing your point range. Basically, the more points you have, the more you bid. With 13-15 points, make a small bid and that could be a pass. With 16-18 points, make a medium-sized bid. With 19-21 points, bid a game contract in your fit (4 Hearts, 4 Spades or 3 Notrump if your fit is in a minor suit).

A. RESPONDER RAISED YOUR SUIT SHOWING A FIT

1. Responder gave a single raise showing 6-9 points:
    a. 13-15 points: PASS.
    b. 16-18 points: Invite game by raising your suit one level. You are making a move toward game but leaving it up to partner to decide.
    c. 19-21 points: Jump to game level in your suit (4 Hearts, 4 Spades, or 3NT if minor suit fit). You know there are enough points for a game contract.
2. Responder jumped to the three level in your suit showing a fit and 10-11 points:
    c. 13-14+ points: PASS with 13, bid game with 14 or more. (4H, 4S or 3NT if your fit is in a minor suit.)

BRIDGE LANGUAGE

A pass by the opener after the responder raised his suit says, "Game is out of reach."

The responder raised the opener's suit one level. If the opener then raises it one level, he is saying, "I have 16-18 points. If you have eight or more points, bid game."

If after the responder raises the opener's suit one level, the opener jumps to game level, he is saying, "I have 19 or more points. Game is our level."

If the opener bids game after the responder jumped in his suit, he shows 14 or more points. He is saying, "We have enough for game."

B. OPENER HAS A FIT WITH THE RESPONDER'S SUIT

If the responder did not support your suit, but you have four-card support for the suit he bid–four plus four equals eight. You have found a fit in his suit. At this stage, it does not matter whether it is a major suit or a minor suit. Tell partner about your fit by raising his suit. Remember to add dummy points if it is a major suit fit. You may think it odd for the opener to add dummy points, but if your partner mentions the suit first, you will be the dummy. The size of your raise shows your point range.

1. Raising a suit responder bid at the one level:
    a. 13-15 points: Raise his suit one level.
    b. 16-18 points: Jump one level in his suit.
    c. 19-21 points: Jump to game level in his suit (4 Hearts, 4 Spades or 3 Notrump if his suit is a minor suit)

BRIDGE LANGUAGE

Opener's raise of the responder's one level suit says, "We have a fit in your suit. The size of my bid shows my point range. The smallest possible raise shows 13-15 points, a medium raise shows 16-18 points, and a jump to game shows 19-21 points"

If responder bid his suit at the two level, it is only a matter of adding points to see if there are enough combined points for a game contract. Remember, when he bid a new suit at the two level, he promised at least 10 points. If you have a fit and can count 25 points, bid game (4Hearts, 4 Spades, 3 Notrump if your fit is in a minor suit). If you can't count enough points for a game, raise his suit one level. He will take it from there.

Sometimes, a slam is possible, but for now, concentrate on getting to a game contract if you have 25 or more combined points. After you are comfortable with this bidding, you will begin to see when you should consider investigating for slam.

OPENER'S REBID WHEN A FIT HAS NOT BEEN FOUND

It is time for your second bid and a fit has not been found. At this time, many openers begin to wonder what the responder holds in his hand. This is not the time to wonder about responder's hand. It is the time to do what the responder is counting on you to do. As far as you know, you are still searching for a fit. Responder wants more information. You will give him the information he needs if you complete the description of your hand (the shape of your hand and point count). Then, he can guide your partnership to a good contract.

If responder bid a new suit or jumped to 2 Notrump, you may not pass as these responses are forcing. He has asked you for more information. You must bid again. If he responded 1 Notrump, he did not ask you for more information. He made that bid simply to keep the auction alive. It was not a forcing bid.

The size of your bid will show your point count (where in your original 13-21 point range your hand belongs). A balanced hand is shown by making your rebid in Notrump (with only one exception). An unbalanced hand is ALWAYS shown by making your rebid in a suit.

OPENER'S REBID WITH A BALANCED HAND

A. WITH 13-14 HIGH CARD POINTS:
1. Bid a new suit at the one level (the one exception to to making a notrump rebid with a balanced hand). Finding a fit takes priority over showing hand shape.
2. With no suit to bid at the one level, make the lowest possible Notrump bid.
   a. Pass if the responder bid 1 Notrump.
   b. Bid 1 Notrump if the responder bid a suit at the one level and you cannot bid a new suit.
   c. Bid 2 Notrump if the responder bid a suit at the two level.
   d. Bid 3 Notrump if the responder made a forcing bid by jumping to 2 Notrump.
B. WITH 15-17 HIGH CARD POINTS: You would have opened 1 Notrump.

C. WITH 18-19 HIGH CARD POINTS:

1. If the responder bid a new suit at the one level, jump to 2 Notrump.
2. If the responder bid 1 Notrump, jump to 3 Notrump.
3. If responder bid a new suit at the two level, jump to 3 Notrump.
4. If the responder jumped to 2 Notrump, it was a forcing bid. This promised a balanced hand and 13-15 points. Bid 3NT. Later you will learn how to investigate for slam. Be satisfied with a game contract for now.

D. WITH 20-21 HIGH CARD POINTS: You would have opened 2 Notrump.

BRIDGE LANGUAGE

If responder bids a new suit at the one level, he is saying, "My hand may be balanced or unbalanced but assume it contains 13-15 points."

If responder bid 1 Notrump, and opener passes, he is saying, "My hand is balanced with 13-14 points."

A rebid in Notrump by the opener says, "My hand is balanced. The size of my bid gives my point range. If I passed your 1Notrump bid or made the smallest bid possible in Notrump, it shows 13-14. A jump in Notrump shows 18-19."

OPENER'S REBID WITH AN UNBALANCED HAND AND NO FIT WITH PARTNER

If responder bid a new suit or bid 1 Notrump and your hand is unbalanced, you must make your rebid in a SUIT. If you have another suit of four or more cards, it is your first choice. Without another four-card or longer suit, rebid your original suit of SIX or more cards. When you rebid a suit, you are promising six cards in that suit.

OPENER'S REBID OF A NEW SUIT OF FOUR OR MORE CARDS

At this point, you do not know what the responder holds in his hand but his bid of a new suit asked for more information. Don't worry about what his hand holds, just finish the description of your hand. He will tell you about his hand on his next bid. You, the opener, are the describer. Just do your job.

Your hand is unbalanced and you have another suit of four or more cards. Perhaps partner also has four cards in that suit. First, decide if your second suit is higher or lower in rank than the suit you originally bid. Suits, you'll recall, are ranked for bidding purposes in alphabetical order—C-D-H-S. Clubs are the lowest in rank and Spades are the highest. After you have decided if your second suit is higher or lower in rank than your original suit, determine in what range of points your hand belongs:

13-15 points – small 16-18 points – medium 19-21 points – Large

POINT REQUIREMENTS FOR NEW SUIT BIDS

A. WITH 13-18 points:

1. The bid of a new suit at the one level:

   a. Responder won't know if your hand is balanced or unbalanced and must assume you have 13-15 points although you could have as many as 18. Unfortunately, it is not always possible to tell partner you have 16-18 points.

2. The bid of a new suit lower in rank than your original suit at the two level:

   a. This shows an unbalanced hand with 5 or more cards in your first suit and four or more in your second suit.

   b. Responder must assume you have 13-15 points although you could have as many as 18. It is not always possible to tell partner you have 16-18 points.

3. If partner responded at the one level, YOU MAY NOT take the bidding to the two level in a new suit higher in rank than the suit you originally bid without 16 or more points. With 13-15, rebid your first suit even if it is only a five card suit. (Normally, you need six cards to rebid a suit but you are in a bind.)

4. If partner has already taken the bidding to the two level, he promised at least 10 points. You may bid a suit higher in rank than your original suit, but it is recommended you have at least 15 Points to do so. With fewer than 15 points, rebid your first suit of five or more cards.

B. WITH 16 or more points:

1. If YOU must take the bidding to the two level (partner responded at the one level), and your second suit is higher in rank than the suit you originally bid, you have enough points to bid it. Doing so is called a REVERSE and it is forcing for one round of bidding (explanation to follow).

C. WITH 19 or more points:

1. Jump one level in a new suit. This is called a JUMP SHIFT because you are jumping one level and shifting to a new strain. A jump shift is FORCING until a game contract is reached.

2. If your hand fits the description for a reverse and YOU must take the bidding to the two level (responder bid a new suit at the one level), you do not need to jump shift as a reverse is forcing.

DISCUSSION OF THE REVERSE BID

Hold on to your hat, this isn't going to be easy. Let's review the requirements for making a REVERSE BID:

1. An unbalanced hand with two suits of unequal length.
2. The lower ranking suit is longer. (remember suits are ranked C-D-H-S).

3. 16+ points
4. You open in the lower ranking suit because it is longer (this is correct).

Here is how it works: Let's say you have an unbalanced hand with 5 cards in Clubs and 4 cards in Diamonds. By following the guidelines for choosing an opening suit, the lower-ranking Club suit is opened because it is longer. So far, so good. If the responder bids 1 Heart or 1 Spade or 1 Notrump, YOU must take the bidding to the two level in order to bid your higher-ranking Diamond suit. With 16+ points, that does not pose a problem. You simply bid 2 Diamonds. Without 16+ points, your hand is not strong enough to make this forcing bid. Holding only 13-15 points, what do you do? If your Club suit were six cards long, the answer would be easy. You would simply rebid your Club suit (when you rebid a suit, you normally promise six cards). The rebid of your suit at the two level shows 13-15 points. But, your Club suit is only five cards long. Your hand isn't strong enough to take the bidding to the two level in your higher ranking Diamond suit, and your original suit isn't long enough to rebid. You are caught between a rock and a hard place, but you must make a choice. Rebid your five-card Club suit. It is the best you can do. At least, your partner will know your hand is unbalanced with a point count of 13-15. This is a safeguard the bidding experts have put into place to prevent the bidding from getting out of control without enough points.

The reverse is always a difficult concept for the beginning player but it is important. You will probably struggle with it for awhile. In the beginning, you'll make many reverse bids when you shouldn't simply because it is an easy mistake to make. After paying the consequences a few times, it will become clear why 16+ points are necessary for this forcing bid.

BRIDGE LANGUAGE

When the opener bids a new suit at the one level, he is saying, "I have at least four cards in this suit. My hand may be balanced or unbalanced. Assume I have 13-15 points."

When the opener bids a suit lower in rank than his original suit at the two level, he is saying, "I have an unbalanced hand with at least five cards in my first suit and four cards in this suit. Assume I have 13-15 points."

When the opener takes the bidding to the two level in a suit higher in rank than his original suit, he is saying, "I have an unbalanced hand with at least five cards in my first suit and four cards in this suit and 16 or more points. You must bid at least one more time."

When the opener jumps in a new suit, he is saying, "I have an unbalanced hand with at least five cards in my first suit and at least four cards in this suit and 19 or more points. This bid is forcing. We can not stop until a game contract has been reached."

If the RESPONDER has already taken the bidding to the two level in a new suit, he has promised ten points. The point requirement for bidding a higher-ranking suit at the two level can be relaxed somewhat, but it is a good idea to have at least 15 points. Otherwise, rebid your five card or longer lower ranking suit.

When you (the opener) have 19 or more points and partner has responded to you, you know he has at least six points. There are enough combined points to bid a game. If you do not know which game you should be playing, you can't risk making a bid that would allow your partner to pass. Make a forcing bid. This could be either a reverse or a jump shift. If your hand fits the description for a reverse, reverse rather than jump shifting. This saves bidding space you may need if slam becomes a possibility.

The bid of a new suit by the responder is forcing. However, the bid of a new suit by the opener is not always forcing. It is only forcing if you (the opener) take the bidding to the two level in a suit higher in rank than your first suit or jump shift in a new suit. Let's repeat that loudly –THE BID OF A NEW SUIT BY THE OPENER IS NOT ALWAYS FORCING. IT IS ONLY FORCING IF YOU (THE OPENER) TAKE THE BIDDING TO THE TWO LEVEL IN A SUIT HIGHER IN RANK THAN YOUR FIRST SUIT OR JUMP SHIFT IN A NEW SUIT.

A. WITH AN UNBALANCED HAND AND NO NEW SUIT TO BID, REBID YOUR ORIGINAL SIX CARD OR LONGER SUIT:

1. 13-15 points: Rebid your suit at the lowest possible level.
2. 16-18 points: Jump to the three level in your suit.
3. 19-21 points: Jump to game level in your suit (4Hearts, 4Spades, 3NT if your suit is a minor). You would be very unlucky if partner did not have at least one card in your suit.

Because the rebid of your original suit simply gives the responder information (six cards, unbalanced hand, point range), it is not a forcing bid. The responder will take this information, add it to what is in his hand and decide whether to pass or continue on.

BRIDGE LANGUAGE

When the opener rebids his original suit, He is saying, "My hand is unbalanced with at least six cards in my suit. The size of my bid shows my point count. Small bid shows 13-15, medium bid shows 16-18 and a game level bid shows 19-21 points."

OPENER'S REBID WITH AN UNBALANCED HAND WHEN RESPONDER HAS JUMPED TO 2NT

When the responder jumped to 2 Notrump, he promised a balanced hand and 13-15 high card points. This bid guaranteed at least two cards in each of the four suits and is forcing until a game is reached.

1. Jump to game level in your six-card major suit. You know you have an eight card fit and enough points for a game contract.
2. If you do not have a six card major suit, bid a new suit of four or more cards or bid 3NT.

EXERCISES

This is a very important chapter and a very difficult one. However, it is vital that you, the opener, give your partner correct information. Shuffle and deal four hands. Choose the hands you would open one-in-a-suit. With these hands, decide in which suit you would open and assume your partner has shown at least six points by responding. Decide what you would do if he showed a fit—raised you one level or jumped in your suit. If he did not show a fit, what would you do if he bid a new suit or 1 Notrump or if he jumped to 2 Notrump? Keep this chapter close by so you can check your answers. Again, it is very helpful if you do this with a partner.

REVIEW OF OPENER'S REBID

1. Remember who you are in the auction and prepare to give a further description of your hand.
2. You may not pass a forcing bid by the responder. If he bid a new suit or jumped to 2 Notrump, he has made a forcing bid. You may pass 1 Notrump if you have a balanced hand with 13-14 points.
3. If you have a fit with your partner, the search for a fit is over be it a major suit fit or a minor suit fit.

All you need to communicate is your point range. Remember to add dummy points if raising your partner's major suit.

4. Without a fit, both your point range and hand shape should be communicated if possible.

5. With a balanced hand and no fit, you usually make a bid in Notrump. There is one exception. With a 13-14 point balanced hand and a new suit that can be bid at the one level, bid the suit. Unfortunately, responder won't know the shape of your hand but finding a fit takes priority.

6. With an unbalanced hand and no fit, your second bid is made in a suit. It is either the bid of a new suit of four or more cards or the rebid of your original six-card suit. (Sometimes, you are desperate and have to rebid a five card suit instead of reversing without enough points.)

7. Bidding a new suit at the one level or a suit lower in rank than your original suit at the two level could show anywhere from 13-18 points. Your partner must assume you have 13-15 points, but it is the best you can do. It is not forcing.

8. A reverse happens when the bidding is still at the one level and YOU, the opener, take the bidding to the two level in a suit that is higher in rank than your original suit. It absolutely guarantees 16 or more points and is forcing for one round.

9. A jump shift is jumping one level on the bidding scale in a new suit. It shows an unbalanced hand

with at least 19 points. It forces your partner to continue bidding until a game contract has been reached. If your hand fits the requirements for the reverse, there is no need to jump shift. Reverse on this bid and show extra strength on subsequent bids.
10. A jump to 2 Notrump shows 18-19 high card points and a balanced hand.

To recap, if you have found a fit, bid according to the number of points you hold (add dummy points if you are raising responder's major suit). If you have not found a fit, bid according to your point count and hand shape. Make your rebid in Notrump if your hand is balanced (except with 13-14 points and a new suit which can be bid at the one level). If your hand is unbalanced, your rebid is always made in a suit—either a new suit of four or more cards or the rebid of your original suit (which usually promises six cards in your suit).

Before you bid a new suit, be aware of whether your second suit is higher or lower in rank than your original suit. If it is lower in rank, you may bid your second suit at the one or two level with 13-18 points. If it is higher in rank, you may bid it at the one level with 13 or more points. However, if YOU must take the bidding to the two level, you need 16 or more points. Without 16 points, repeat your first suit of five or more cards at the two level. If responder has already taken the bidding to the two level, you may bid your higher ranking suit but it is a good idea to have 15 points. Otherwise, repeat your first suit of five or more cards.

With 19 or more points, bid game if you know where to bid it. If not, make a forcing bid. This may be a reverse if you hand qualifies or a jump shift (both bids are forcing).

RESPONDER'S REBID

Your partner opened the bidding with one in a suit, you responded, and he has made his second bid. The good news is, you, the responder, often realizes the best contract has already been reached and can pass. The bad news is, you can't count on it. But, if opener gave you a true description of his hand and you listened, you now have a good picture of his hand. It is up to you to decide where the hand is going. If the final contract has not been decided, it will likely be set with your rebid.

Many things need to be taken into consideration before you make your rebid. It is going to take some time and effort to become proficient. Don't expect perfection. Even if you do everything right, there is no guarantee of finding the best contract all the time. Many factors affect the outcome of a particular hand, including the element of luck. Do the best you can with the facts you have and most of the time, a suitable contract can be found.

Remember, this is a partnership game. Not only should you allow yourself to make mistakes, but you should extend the same courtesy to your partner. If you forgive his mistakes, he is more inclined to overlook yours. In the game of Bridge, there is nothing sweeter than playing with a happy partner.

That said, let's try to decide the best course of action. Be aware of your point count, add dummy points if they apply, and place your hand in one of these point ranges:

> 6-9 points....................small hand
> 10-11 points...............medium hand
> 12 or more points.........large hand

Try to determine what the opener told you about his hand. Is it balanced or unbalanced? What is his point range? If your partnership has found a fit, your only concern is the number of combined points.

THE OPENER HAS SHOWN 13-15 POINTS

A. Opener made the lowest bid possible when he:
  1. Bid a new suit at the one level—his hand may be balanced or unbalanced. You should assume he has 13-15 points although he could have as many as 18.
  2. Bid a lower ranking suit at the two level—his hand is unbalanced. This shows five+ cards in his first suit and four+ in his second suit. You must assume he

has 13-15 points although he could have as many as 18.

3. Raised the responder's suit one level. He has 13-15 points.

4. Rebid his own suit at the two level–his hand is unbalanced and almost always promises six cards in his suit. He has 13-15 points.

5. Made the lowest possible bid in Notrump–his hand is balanced with 13-14 points.

With all these rebids by the opener, you must assume he has 13-15 points. If you also have a small hand of 6-9 points, the possibility of scoring a game contract is so remote you shouldn't even consider it. Your job now is to find the best part score contract and sign off at a low level. Remember, a trump suit is very helpful with few points.

RESPONDER'S REBID WITH 6-9 POINTS WHEN OPENER HAS SHOWN SMALL HAND

1. Pass if you have a fit with the opener's second suit or he raised your suit one level.

2. If you concealed a minor suit fit on your first bid, bid it at the two level.

3. Rebid your own six-card suit at the two level.

4. If the opener bid a lower-ranking suit at the two level and you have no six-card suit of your own, choose one of his suits. Make the choice by selecting the suit in which your partnership has the most cards. He

has shown an unbalanced hand which promises five cards in his first suit and four in his second. Add the number of your cards to his. With more cards in his second suit, pass. With more cards in his first suit, bid it at the two level. If you have seven in both, prefer the 5-2 fit to the 4-3 fit.

5. If the bidding is still at the one level and you have no fit or six-card suit of your own, bid 1 Notrump or pass the opener's 1 Notrump rebid.

When you know there are not enough combined points to bid a game contract, you want to stop at a low level. You also want to play in a trump contract if possible. A trump suit gives weak hands some strength they would not have in a Notrump contract. In the choices 1-4 above, you are helping your partnership by placing the contract in a trump suit. If you are able to make one of the first four choices, do so. Number 5 is your last choice since the hand must be played in Notrump. However, if that is your only choice, that is your only choice.

Deciding what to do when opener has shown a small hand (13-15) and responder also has a small hand is probably the responder's most difficult rebid. However, it is often the rebid you have to make. Study the responses above to know what your options are.

RESPONDER'S REBID WITH 10-11 POINTS WHEN OPENER HAS SHOWN A SMALL HAND OF 13-15 POINTS

When the opener has shown a small hand and you, the responder, have 10-11 points, a game contract is possible if the opener has at least 14 points. Ask him by:

1. Raising opener's suit to the three level with a fit.
2. Raising your own six-card suit to the three level.
3. Without a fit or a six-card suit of your own, bid 2 Notrump to invite game This bid does not promise a balanced hand and is not forcing. It is just a way to tell partner you have no fit but you have 10-11 points and are inviting him to bid game with 14 points.
4. Raising opener's 1 Notrump rebid to 2 Notrump with 11 points.

These bids make a move toward game without actually bidding it. In other words, they extend an invitation to the opener to bid game if he has 14 or more points. The opener should recognize these bids as invitational because they are not responses made with 6-9 points. With 13 points, opener passes. He bids game with 14 or more points.

RESPONDER'S REBID WITH 12 OR MORE POINTS AND OPENER HAS PROMISED 13-15 POINTS

With 12 or more points, you know your partnership belongs in at least a game contract. He had 13 points to open the bidding. If your hand is very strong, there may be a possibility of a slam. For now, concentrate on bidding a game contract.

1. Pass, if a game has already been bid by your partnership.
2. Bid 4 Hearts, 4 Spades with a major suit fit or 3NT with minor suit fit.
3. If you do not know which game to bid, bid a new four card or longer suit at the three level for more information.

RESPONDER'S REBID WHEN OPENER HAS SHOWN MEDIUM HAND OF 16-18 POINTS

The opener has shown a medium hand by jumping in his original six-card suit, jumping in the responder's suit or raising his original suit after responder gave him a single raise. Responder's options are:

6-7 Points –Pass
With 8 or more points:

1. With a fit: Bid game (4Hearts, 4 Spades or 3 NT if fit is in a minor suit).
2. Without a fit: Bid a new suit at the three level to get more information or if you know a major suit fit is impossible, bid 3NT.

OPENER HAS REVERSED

A reverse bid by the opener showed at least 16 points, but he could have as many as 21. Passing is out of the question because this bid is forcing for one round of bidding. Your options as responder are;

With 6-8 points:

1. Bid a suit that has already been bid by the partnership at the lowest level possible. Repeat of your suit may be done with a five card suit (in this situation, it does not promise six).
2. Bid 2 Notrump

With 9 or more points:

1. Bid a game contract if you know which game.
2. Bid a new suit to get more information.

OPENER HAS SHOWN A LARGE HAND OF 19-21 POINTS

Opener has shown a maximum hand by jump shifting or bidding game. If he jump shifted in a suit, make sure your partnership gets to a game contract even with only six points. Bid game if you know where or bid a new suit for more information. If he jumped to 2 Notrump showing a balanced hand and 18-19 points, you usually get to game but with very weak 6 points, you may pass.

A. If opener jump-shifted in a new suit or bid game.
   1. Pass if the contract is already at game level.
   2. Bid a game contract if you know where it belongs.
   3. If you are still unsure, bid a new suit to get more information.
B. If opener jumped to 2 Notrump and you have decided there are enough combined points for game:
   1. Bid game in your major suit with six cards.
   2. Rebid your major suit at the three level with five cards. He could have three cards in your suit and if so, he will choose the major suit game. With only two cards, he bids 3NT.
   3. Without 5 or more cards in your major suit, bid 3 Notrump.

DECIDING TO BID A SLAM

If you bid a game contract and take 12 or 13 tricks, you win trick points for all tricks taken and game bonus points. If you bid and make a slam, the bonus points are even larger. However, if you bid a slam and don't fulfill your contract, you receive no points, and your opponents are awarded penalty points for all under tricks. The point is, if you bid and make a slam, you are rewarded handsomely, but if you fail to make it, you give up all the points you would have scored by stopping at game level.

As you can see, there is a certain amount of risk involved in slam bidding. This book does not discuss slam bidding in depth, but because you are probably anxious to give it a try, here are a couple of suggestions.

You need 33 points for a small slam and 37 points for a grand slam. Later you will learn sophisticated methods of determining exact point counts or locating specific control cards (Aces and Kings). If you can count 33 or more points, bid a small slam. For now, don't even consider bidding a grand slam (taking all 13 tricks). Bidding a grand slam is risky even for expert players. Be satisfied with a small slam.

Slams are easier to play with a trump suit, so, if you have located a major or minor suit fit, play the slam in a suit contract. If considering a slam, and your fit is in a minor suit, add dummy points if you are the dummy. When a contract is being played using a minor suit as a trump suit, short suits are an advantage. Game contracts in minor suits are played in 3 Notrump, and short suits are not an asset because you do not have a trump suit. Therefore, you did not add dummy points.

WHEN THE AUCTION BECOMES A CONTEST

U ntil now we have discussed auctions where only one partnership has entered the bidding. Does that mean the other partnership isn't allowed to bid? Unfortunately, that would happen only in a perfect world. Competitive bidding is commonplace in bidding auctions, and makes the auction more difficult.

Is it worthwhile for a second partnership to get into the auction when their opponents have already announced strength? After all, there are only so many points to go around, and the opener (and perhaps his partner) has acknowledged owning a good chunk of them. When you enter the auction as an opening bidder, you are hoping to find a game contract or better. If you come into the auction after the opposition has made a bid, you do so with a different attitude.

You realize it is highly unlikely (but not impossible) your partnership can reach a game contract and the possibility of a slam is almost nonexistent. You will probably be competing for a part-score contract. Perhaps this makes competing for the contract hardly seem worthwhile, but quite often it is a very good idea. The reasons you want to compete are:

1. To win the contract. You will probably be pleased to win a part-score contract, but maybe you will find enough points to bid a game (rarely a slam). There are no large bonuses given for part-score contracts, but why shouldn't you compete for the trick points? You may be entitled to win them.
2. To interfere with the opponents' bidding: If they must bid in an unfamiliar way, it won't be so easy for them to find the right contract. Competing has a nuisance value because it uses space on the bidding scale.
3. To push them higher. In order to win the contract, they may be willing to bid higher than they can afford.
4. You may cause them to not bid high enough.
5. To give your partner information: Your bid gives your partner a good idea of what to lead. This is called LEAD DIRECTING.

Even if you can't win the contract, why let your opponents skip down the garden path to an easy contract? If they are allowed to bid their contract in a familiar way, the chances are they will make the right decisions. If you enter the auction and go down, you won't lose much because the opponents would have scored points anyway.

There is an unusual twist to this. The partnership opening the bidding may continue, hoping to win the contract, or they may decide it would be more advantageous to get out of the auction and defend the hand. If you win the contract but fail to fulfill it, you are penalized.

Your opponents can increase your penalties by saying DOUBLE after your bid. The penalties are doubled if you fail to make a doubled contract, which can be rather costly if you don't have something to back up your bid. This is a good reason to think before entering the auction. A double is erased if someone makes another bid, but stands if there are three passes in a row.

There is another reason to think before becoming a competitive bidder. On each deal, your partnership is classified as being either VULNERABLE or NONVULNERABLE. The bonus points for making a contract are much greater when you are vulnerable, but the penalties for failing are also greater. If you are opening the bidding, you need not concern yourself with vulnerability, but when thinking about becoming a competitive bidder, consider the meaning of vulnerable. You are in the position of being wounded or severely damaged. If your opponents double your contract, you can suffer enormous penalties. Check your vulnerability before you enter into a competitive auction. If you are

thinking of competing just to interfere with your opponents, think twice. It may not be worth the risk.

Are you wondering how you know when you are vulnerable and when you are not vulnerable? Your vulnerability is known before the hand is dealt and has nothing
to do with a particular hand. On some hands, neither
partnership is vulnerable, while on other hands only one
partnership is. Sometimes both partnerships are vulnerable. It depends on the type of Bridge you are playing.
The vulnerability for each hand and each partnership has
been decided before the game begins if you are playing
duplicate or four-hand Bridge. In Rubber Bridge, you
are vulnerable after you have scored a game toward your
rubber. If in doubt, ask the players at your table before
you bid.

When the opponents have opened the bidding, it isn't
necessary to always take action. Bid only if you have
something to say. Exercise caution when you are vulnerable. It is especially important to pass if they open
in one of your strong suits. In this situation, it is wise
to defend the hand. Lie in the weeds and wait for them
to reach a high level and then double their contract for
penalty. Experience helps you decide when silence is
golden and when a bid is better.

There are two competitive actions you may be able
to take. One way to compete is to OVERCALL and the
other is to make a TAKEOUT DOUBLE. We are going
to look at each of these separately.

OVERCALLS

When the opponents open the bidding and you come in to make a bid in a suit or in Notrump, you are competing for the contract. You are called the OVERCALLER because you are making a bid or a call over the opponents' bid. Your partner is known as the ADVANCER. An overcall can be made at any level on the bidding scale. In this book, we are considering overcalls made at the cheapest possible level. These are called a SIMPLE OVERCALLS. Learn simple overcalls first and add more complicated ones to your game later. The old crawl before you walk idea again.

Just as the opener had to meet certain requirements before opening the bidding, the overcaller must meet certain requirements before making an overcall. These requirements are not the same as those of the opener. All suits (Clubs, Diamonds, Hearts and Spades) positively require at least FIVE cards to be considered for an overcall. If the overcall is made at the two level, it generally promises at least 13 points and it is a good idea to have a six card or longer suit. You can be slightly more relaxed about a one-level overcall. Nine points (experienced players do it with less) and a good suit are good rules of thumb. With two suits that fit the overcall requirements, bid the longer first or the higher ranking if they are tied in length.

Your suit should be a good one to qualify for an overcall. It is a good idea to have at least two of the following in your suit:

1. Ace
2. King
3. Queen
4. Jack and Ten (treat as one unit)

This probably sounds like Face Card Hang-Up, but an overcaller does not make the same promise as an opener. An opening suit may be of any quality, but an overcalled suit promises strength. Remember that an overcall is lead directing and your partner is almost certain to lead your suit. Be prepared to take some tricks in your suit or you will have a very unhappy partner on your hands. Along with at least five cards, an overcalled suit promises some high-card strength in that suit. If your suit is longer than five cards, you may relax the high card requirement somewhat.

BRIDGE LANGUAGE

A simple overcall says, "I have a good suit and I have at least five cards in my suit. If I overcalled at the one level, I have 9-17 points. If I overcalled at the two level, I usually have a 6+ card suit or a very good 5 card suit and 13-17 points."

An overcall may also be made in Notrump. The requirements for a 1 Notrump overcall are very much like those of a 1 Notrump opening bid: You must have a balanced hand in the 15-18 high card point range and you also MUST have a stopper in the opponents' bid suit. A stopper is strength in the suit or suits bid by the opponents. Some examples of stoppers are: A, Kx, QJ10, Qxxx, QJxx.

It is almost guaranteed the opposition will lead the suit they bid. If you do not have a way to stop them from running that suit, you are in trouble. In a Notrump contract, you do not have a trump suit and must find another way to protect yourself. A stopper in their suit is your protection. Without a stopper, it is best to stay out of the auction and defend the hand. Perhaps you will have the opportunity to double them for penalty.

BRIDGE LANGUAGE
A 1 Notrump overcall says, "I have a balanced hand with 15-18 points and some strength in the opponent's bid suit."

Responses to suit overcalls are very similar to responses to opening bids in a suit. Keep in mind you need only three cards to have an eight-card fit in your partner's overcalled suit regardless of the suit he named (Clubs, Diamonds, Hearts or Spades).

ADVANCER'S RESPONSES WITH A FIT IN PARTNER'S SUIT OVERCALL
1. Raise one level with 8-9 points. If he overcalled at the two level, pass with fewer than 8 points.
2. CUE BID the opponent's suit (bid the opponent's suit) to show you have a fit and 10+points. If the overcaller made his overcall with less than opening

point count, he rebids his suit at the lowest level or passes if the opponent comes in to make a bid before him. Any other rebid by the overcaller shows full opening point count.

3. If your fit is in a minor suit, have a stopper in the opener's suit before bidding 3 Notrump.
4. Responses to 1 Notrump overcalls are similar to responses to 1 Notrump opening bids which are discussed in the last three chapters of this book.

If you do not have three-card support for your partner's suit, you may bid a new suit. It is a good idea to have at least five cards in any new suit you bid. Most partnerships consider a new suit by an unpassed advancer as a forcing bid. The overcaller MUST bid again. Your partnership may decide a change of suit is not forcing, but make sure you have that agreement before playing.

If you do not have three card support for your partner's suit and can't bid a new suit, consider a Notrump bid, but you need some strength in the opponents' suit to do this.

1. Pass with 6-7 points.
2. Bid 1 Notrump with 8-10 points and a stopper in the opponents' suit.
3. Bid 2 Notrump with 11-12 points and a stopper.
4. Bid 3 Notrump with 13 points and a stopper

HANDS FOR OVERCALLS

Your Right Hand Opponent (RHO) opened the bidding at 1 Diamond and these are hands you may hold.

	1.	2.	3.	4.	5.
Spades	Kxxxx	xxx	AQx	KJX	Axx
Hearts	Qxx	AKJxx	KQJx	Ax	Kxx
Diamonds	xx	xx	KQx	xx	AJ10xx
Club	Ax	Qxx	xxx	AQJxxxx	Jx

Answers:

1. Pass. You do not have a suit that qualifies.
2. Overcall 1 Heart. Your suit is a good one and you are at the one level.
3. Overcall 1 Notrump. Your hand is balanced with 17 high card points and you have a stopper.
4. Overcall 2 Clubs. You have the strength of an opening hand and a good six-card suit.
5. Pass. The opponent bid your strong suit. Maybe you will have the opportunity to double for penalty.

TAKEOUT DOUBLE

What do you do if you would like to get into the auction, but you do not have a good five-card suit? Is there any way you can compete for the contract? Yes. Bidding experts devised the TAKEOUT DOUBLE, and this bid gives you a way to compete even when your hand does not fit the requirements for an overcall.

Years ago, all doubles were made for penalties. In other words, when you thought your opponent could not fulfill his contract, you said, "Double." If he failed to make his contract, his penalty points were doubled. Times have changed. Today, a double may be for penalty or it may be a takeout double that says, "Partner, take the contract out of this double and put it in your best suit." It is a way to bid three suits for the price of one bid and it is quite a bargain. You show the point count of an opening hand, but allow your partner to choose one of the unbid suits. You are known as the DOUBLER and your partner is the ADVANCER.

Of course, you can't double for takeout unless your hand meets certain requirements. That would be bidding suicide. The doubler needs:

1. Point value of an opening hand (13 points). Check below to determine how to count your points.
2. It is a good idea to have no more than two cards in the opponents' bid suit.
3. At least three cards in all the unbid suits.

You may be able to make a takeout double with a hand that would have been too weak to open the bidding. How is this possible? When you count your points to make an opening bid, you are not sure of any fit and can't take your short suits (voids, singletons, doubletons) into consideration. When you double, you guarantee at least a seven card fit in any suit your partner names (remember, you promise three cards in all the unbid suits). If he names the suit, who is going to be the dummy? That's right, you are. Add dummy points when you value your hand. Partner is going to give preference to major suits.

Ideally, the doubler would always promise four cards in each of the unbid suits. This would guarantee an eight-card fit with any suit his partner named. However, it is rare to be dealt such a perfect hand and if you wait around for perfection, you may never compete. The promise the takeout doubler makes is at least three cards in each of the unbid suits. You may end up playing in a seven-card fit, but Bridge, just as life, isn't always perfect.

The words takeout and penalty are not on the Bridge vocabulary list and you are not allowed to announce just what your double means. Your partner must figure it out for himself. Here are some ways to make the distinction:

1. If this is your partnership's first chance to bid and the contract is at a low level on the bidding scale, the double is for takeout.
2. If the contract is at a low level and neither you nor your partner has said anything other than pass, it is for takeout.
3. If either you or your partner has made a bid other than pass, the double is for penalty.
4. The opponents' contract is a suit contract. The double of a 1 Notrump opening bid is for penalty (unless you have added some conventions to your game).
5. Doubles of game contracts are for penalty.

BRIDGE LANGUAGE

Doubling a SUIT bid by the opponents at a low level when neither the doubler nor his partner has made a previous bid (except pass), is for takeout. The doubler is saying, "I have an opening point hand with at least three cards in each of the unbid suits. Bid your best suit giving preference to major suits. This bid is forcing."

The takeout double is a forcing bid. If you are the doubler's partner, it commands you to take the contract out of the double by placing your partnership in one of the unbid suits. You may not pass (even with zero points) unless your right-hand opponent bids and erases the double. Does this sound scary to you? You would probably hate to bid with 0-5 points, wouldn't you? Don't be afraid. Actually, you are no worse off than when your partner opens the bidding and you have no points. In fact, you are in a better position. If your partnership is left to play the contract, at least you will have a trump fit.

ADVANCER'S RESPONSES TO A TAKEOUT DOUBLE

1. 0-5 points: Unlike responding to an opening bid, your partner is forcing you to respond. Bid your longest unbid suit at the lowest possible level. Prefer a four card major to a five-card minor. If your right hand opponent makes a bid before you, he has erased the double. In that case, you are off the hook and can pass.

2. 6-8 points: Bid your longest unbid suit at the lowest level possible. Prefer a four-card major to a five-card minor. Bid even if your RHO (right-hand opponent) bids before you. If you bid after your opponent has

bid and erased the double, you are making a FREE BID. When you make a free bid, your partner will count on you for at least six points. If your RHO did not bid before you, you may bid twice in the auction to show partner you are not completely broke.

3. 9-11 points: Invite game by jumping a level in your suit. Your partner promised a fit and you are just showing your point count.

4. 12+ points: Jump to game in your major suit. With two four card majors, cue bid the opponent's suit (bid his suit). This cue bid promises 12+ points and asks the doubler to choose the major suit he would like.

Be sure to bid something when your partner makes a takeout double unless your hand has 0-5 points and your RHO bids before you. You have a guaranteed fit and you are simply naming your best suit and showing your partner your point count. He wants a bid from you. Be a good partner and comply with his wishes.

The doubler is looking for a suit and that is always preferable to a Notrump bid, but if Notrump is the only bid you can make:

    0-10 points.............Bid 1 Notrump
    11-12 points...........Bid 2 Notrump
    13+ points..............Bid 3 Notrump

You need a stopper in the opponent's bid suit to bid Notrump, and that may be length in the opponent's suit.

Once in a blue moon, you are dealt a hand with tremendous strength in the suit the opponent bid (at least five cards headed by a three card honor sequence such as AKQxx, KQJxx. In that case, leave the double in and hope to score more points by defeating their doubled contract. If you leave the double in, your partner MUST lead the opponent's suit.

THE TAKEOUT DOUBLER'S REBID

Exercise caution when making your rebid. Partner's bid told you how he is fixed for points. If it was at the lowest level and was not a free bid, he may have zero points. After all, you forced him into the auction.

13-15 points........Pass unless your partner jumped. If he jumped, bid game with 15 or more points.

16-18 points........Raise one level if his response was at lowest level. Bid game if he jumped.

19-21 points........Jump in his suit if he bid at lowest level. Bid game if he jumped.

As you can see, if partner bid at the lowest level and his bid was not a free bid, you are uncertain of his strength. He could have 0-5 points or he could have 6-8 points. Bid according to your points but bid one level lower than you would have if you had opened and he responded showing at least 6 points. If partner made a free bid or jumped, you know his point range and he has decided the strain of the contract (Clubs, Diamonds, Hearts, Spades or Notrump). Pass, jump, or bid game just as an opener would do when a fit has been found.

Since the upper limit of an overcall is 17 points, you must have a way to show a hand with a 5 card or longer suit and 18 or more points. Here is how you do it. Double first and then bid your 5+ card suit. When you do not accept the suit partner bids, he will realize your hand is stronger and take it from there. With a balanced hand of 19 or more high card points and a stopper in the opponent's suit, double first and bid Notrump on your second bid. Partner will realize your hand was too strong to just overcall 1 Notrump.

You now have the basics for opening at the one level in a suit, responding to one in a suit, opener's and responder's rebids, overcalling and responding to overcalls, the takeout double and responses to that double. We turn now to responding to Notrump opening bids.

RESPONDING
TO A NOTRUMP
OPENING BID

Your partner opened in a Notrump bid. Keep in mind he was not suggesting the hand be played in a Notrump contract. He was simply giving you a very good description of his hand. You are the responder and the goal of finding the best final contract is, once again, your responsibility. You are to take the information the opener gave you and determine the best contract which may or may not be a Notrump contract.

Actually, because of opener's wonderful description, responding to a Notrump opening bid is easier than responding to one-in-a-suit. He has promised a very small range of high card points (15-17 for 1 Notrump and 20-21 for 2 Notrump). He also promised at least two cards in every suit (because his hand is balanced, he cannot have a void or a singleton). The basic responses are discussed first, but because almost all bridge players use the Stayman convention and Jacoby transfers, these conventions have been included in the revision of this book.

BASIC RESPONSES TO A 1 NOTRUMP OPENING BID

Responses to a 1 Notrump opening bid are different from those used when partner opens one-in-a-suit because you have been given different information. His range of high card points is 15-17 and he has promised at least two cards in each suit. Count your points. Count both high card points and long card points. You are going to respond to his Notrump opening bid according to the number of TOTAL points in your hand. Responders worry needlessly about responding with an unbalanced hand. Your hand does not need to be balanced. In fact, responder's hand may be very unbalanced. It is the Notrump opener who promises a balanced hand. When responding to his bid, the responder's hand may be balanced or unbalanced. Don't worry about the shape of your hand. Just count the number of total points in your hand and place that total in one of these three point ranges:

0-7 points (high card points and long card points)
8-9 points (high card points and long card points)
10+ points (high card points and long card points)

Because you are responding to such a small range of points, you can immediately determine if you have enough combined points to reach a game contract, may have enough, or definitely do not enough points for game.

RESPONSES TO 1 NOTRUMP WITH 0-7 POINTS

With simple addition, you can determine you definitely do not have enough points for a game contract when you hold 0-7 points. There is no way you can reach 25 when you hold fewer than eight points. Your contract must be a part score contract. Remember, the fewer combined points you have, the more you want to be in a trump contract. Your partner has promised at least two cards in every suit. You can place him in a trump contract if you hold a five card or longer Diamond, Heart or Spade suit. You have at least a seven card fit (and more likely an eight card fit). Playing in a low level trump contract is much safer than passing 1 Notrump. Bid your five card Diamond, Heart, or Spade suit at the two level. This tells the opener there is no hope for game and that you have placed him in a trump fit which is a better contract. The power of a trump suit will give your weak hand some strength. The trump suit will take tricks that would not have been taken in a Notrump contract. The responses of 2 Diamonds, 2 Hearts or 2 Spades are called signoff bids and they command the opener to pass. These signoff bids are used to rescue your partner from a Notrump contract which would probably fail.

BRIDGE LANGUAGE

In response to a 1 Notrump opening bid, a bid of 2 Hearts, 2 Diamonds or 2 Spades says, "I have added our points and We do not have enough to bid game. This is our best contract. Trust me and pass."

The 2 Club bid is saved for Stayman which you will learn in the next chapter. If your only five card suit happens to be the Club suit, pass. If you have no five card or longer Diamond, Heart or Spade suit, pass. You don't like leaving partner in the 1 Notrump contract but you have no choice.

BRIDGE LANGUAGE

A pass in response to a 1 Notrump opening bid says, "I have 0-7 points and we are playing this hand in a part score contract. A trump fit couldn't be found. Sorry, it must be played in Notrump."

RESPONSES TO 1 NOTRUMP WITH 8-9 POINTS

With eight or nine points, can a game contract be bid? You can't be sure. Your combined point total may or may not be 25 points. For example, (15+9=24) but (17+8=25). It depends on the number of points the opener has. Tell him your point count by bidding 2 Notrump and leave the decision up to him. This does not show a balanced hand. It simply tells opener you have 8-9 points. It says nothing about the shape of your hand.

BRIDGE LANGUAGE

A 2 Notrump response to a 1 Notrump opening bid says, "We are playing this hand in a Notrump contract but I need your help to decide the level. Pass with 15 points. Bid 3 Notrump with 17 points. Use judgment with 16 points. If you have a five card suit or 10's or 9's that may be promoted, bid 3 Notrump. Otherwise, pass.

Until you study more advanced bidding, 2 Notrump is the only response available to you with 8-9 points, and the hand must be played in Notrump. This makes responding to a 1 Notrump opening bid with 8-9 points easy for now.

RESPONSES TO 1 NOTRUMP WITH 10 OR MORE POINTS

A game contract must be reached. Even if the opener has the minimum of 15 points, you are absolutely certain your partnership has 25 points (15+10=25). The only decision left is whether to play the game in a major suit contract or in a Notrump contract. Major suit game contracts are always a priority but you must locate an eight card fit. With six or more cards in one of the major suits (Hearts or Spades), simply jump to the four level (game level) in that suit. Your partner promised at least two cards in all suits so you are guaranteed an eight-card fit. You have all the information you need to set the contract. As the Nike commercial says, "Just do it."

BRIDGE LANGUAGE

In response to a 1 Notrump opening bid, a bid of 4 Hearts or 4 Spades says, "We have at least 25 points and an eight card fit in this major suit. Our final contract is this major suit game."

What if you have five cards in a major suit? An eight-card major suit fit is not only possible, but very likely. The opener has only one doubleton so he is three times more likely to have three or more cards in your suit than to have only two. How do you ask him? You can't respond at the two level in your major because he will pass. You ask by jumping to the three level in your major suit. This is a FORCING BID. He is forced to bid and to choose the best game contract. With three cards in your major, he bids to the four level (game level) in your suit. With only two cards, he bids 3NT. Your jump not only promises a 5 card major, but also ten or more points.

BRIDGE LANGUAGE

In response to a 1 Notrump opening bid, a 3 Heart or 3 Spade bid says, "We have enough points for a game contract, but you must decide which game. I have five cards in this major suit, do you have three? With three cards, bid game in this suit. With only two cards, bid 3 Notrump."

Without a five card or longer major, the game is played in 3 Notrump. Even with a long minor suit, the best game contract is 3 Notrump. You are not interested in playing a 5 Club or 5 Diamond game. Simply bid 3NT.

BRIDGE LANGUAGE

A 3 Notrump response to a 1 Notrump opening bid says, "We have enough points for game but there is no possibility of a major suit game. Our final contract is 3 Notrump."

WHAT THE 1 NOTRUMP OPENER DOES AFTER HIS PARTNER RESPONDS.

The 1 Notrump opener must recognize the responder's bid as a sign off, invitational or forcing bid. If it is a sign-off, the responder has set the final contract and the opener must pass. If it is an invitational bid, the opener has the option of passing or bidding game. If the bid is forcing, the opener may not pass. This is probably not what you want to hear but the only way you can learn these is to memorize them.

RESPONSES TO A 1 NOTRUMP OPENING BID

What do you do if partner makes one of these responses to your 1 Notrump opening bid?

A. Pass...Answer–pass
B. 2 Diamonds, 2 Hearts, 2 Spades........Answer–pass
C. 3 Notrump...Answer–pass
D. 4 Hearts, 4 Spades............................Answer–pass

3. You opened 1 Notrump. What do you do if partner makes one of these responses?

   A. 2 Notrump
       Answer: Pass with 15 points. Bid 3 Notrump with 17 points. With 16 points, use judgment. With a five card suit or 10's or 9's in suits which can be promoted, bid 3 Notrump. Otherwise, pass.

   B. 3 Hearts or 3 Spades
       Answer: Bid at the four level in partner's suit with three cards in his suit. Bid 3 Notrump with only two cards in his suit.

These are the basic responses to 1 Notrump opening bids. There will be times when you have a lot more than ten points and could possibly bid a slam. Slams are contracts at the six and seven level on the bidding scale and award huge bonus points when bid and made. In order to bid them, you need more complex bidding procedures. Venturing into slam bidding is not recommended until you are confident with part-score and game-level bidding. For now, be satisfied to get to a game level contract with 25 or more points. This will hold you in good stead until you are ready to move forward.

Later, you will add some CONVENTIONS to your game. A convention is a bid that means something entirely different than its natural interpretation. A convention is only valid when both partners know it and agree to use it. The two conventions used routinely with Notrump bidding are the STAYMAN CONVENTION and JACOBY TRANSFERS. The last two chapters of this book deal with these conventions. Until you have added these to your game, if someone asks if you play these conventions, just say, "No, not yet."

EXERCISE

1. Take a regular deck of cards and remove a balanced hand with 15-17 high card points and set it aside. Deal out the other three hands and decide how each of these hands would respond to a 1 Notrump opening bid. Keep shuffling and redealing and practice, practice, practice while checking your responses to those listed above.

   a. Remember, you are bidding according to your total point count (high card points and long card points) and you do not need a balanced hand. In fact, your hand may be very unbalanced.

Become comfortable with the bidding thus far and when you think you are ready, it is a very good idea to begin adding conventions to your game.

CONVENTIONS

Bidding conventions are artificial bids that carry definite meanings to a partnership. To use a particular convention, both members of the partnership must agree to do so as these artificial bids do not suggest playing in the strain (Clubs, Diamonds, Hearts, Spades, Notrump) named.

THE STAYMAN CONVENTION AND JACOBY TRANSFERS

The Stayman convention and Jacoby Transfers are two of the most commonly used conventions and are used when responding to Notrump opening bids. The purpose of these conventions is to help you locate an eight card fit in a major suit. You definitely need to add these to your game.

Remember, when your partner opens in a 1 Notrump bid, he is not suggesting the hand be played in a Notrump contract. He is simply giving a very good description of his hand. As always, it is the responder's responsibility to place the partnership in the best contract available.

Because the opener has limited his point range to 15-17, deciding how to respond is easier than responding to an opening one-in-a-suit bid. If responder has zero to seven points, there is no possibility of a game contract and it is always better to play a part score contract with a trump suit (any trump suit). With eight or nine points, a game contract may be possible and a major suit game is a priority. With 10 or more points, responder must make sure a game is reached and again a major suit game is preferred. The Stayman convention and Jacoby transfers help you reach all these goals. They also provide a way to make the Notrump opener the declarer. This will give your partnership a big advantage as it hides opener's strong hand from the opponents making the task of defending much more difficult.

Often times, the Stayman convention is taught and sometime later, Jacoby transfers are added. A better way to learn these conventions is back to back and this is how this book will do it. Stayman is used when you hold at least one FOUR card major or when you hold a four card and a five card major. Jacoby transfers are used when you hold one or two major suits of FIVE or more cards. Jacoby transfers may also be used with a very weak hand holding a six card minor suit. Learning these conventions back to back eliminates learning certain bidding procedures in Stayman you no longer need and have to discard when you add transfers.

While learning Stayman and Major Suit Jacoby transfers, if your hand does not contain a four card or longer major suit, pass with 0-7 points. With 8-9 points, bid 2Notrump. With 10 or more points, bid 3Notrump. With a much stronger hand, you may want to consider investigating for slam. However, for now, just get to game.

THE STAYMAN CONVENTION

The Stayman Convention is used in response to an opening Notrump bid when you hold at least one FOUR card major suit. If you and your partner have agreed to use this convention, the response of 2 Clubs (if partner opened 1 Notrump) asks this question of the opening Notrump bidder, "Do you have a four card or longer major suit?" That is all it asks and it says nothing about the Club suit. Easy, so far?

BRIDGE LANGUAGE

The response of 2Clubs to a 1 Notrump opening bid asks, "Do you have a major suit of four or more cards?"

How does opener answer the question? If he has a four card or longer major suit, he says yes by bidding it at the two level. If he has two four card majors, he bids the lower ranking heart suit at the two level.

BRIDGE LANGUAGE

The response of 2 Hearts says, "I have 4 Hearts." The response of 2 Spades says, I do not have 4 Hearts, but I do have 4 Spades."

With no four card or longer major, he bids 2 Diamonds. This is an artificial bid and says nothing about the Diamond suit. It simply denies a four card major.

BRIDGE LANGUAGE

The response of 2 Diamonds to responder's 2 Club Stayman bid says, "I do not have a four card major suit."

These and only these are the responses the responder wants to hear. Be a good partner and use only the above responses to say yes or no to the Stayman question. By the way, partner is not asking if you have a good four card major–just a four card major. Do not become afflicted with Face Card Hang-Up.

REQUIREMENTS FOR USING THE STAYMAN CONVENTION:

1. You are responding to a Notrump opening bid.
2. Eight or more points if responding to a 1 Notrump opening bid. Count high card points and long card points.
3. One or two FOUR card major suits.
4. May have one four card major and one five card major suit.
5. Without a four card major, five card or longer majors are handled using Jacoby transfers. Transfers are explained in the next chapter.

6. If your partner opened 2 Notrump (20-21 points) or 2Clubs–then 2 Notrump (22-24 points), you may use Stayman but Clubs are bid at the three level. Fewer points are needed because you are responding to a different point range.

After the opener gives his yes or no answer to your Stayman question, it is time to tell him the strength of your hand. How you do this depends on whether or not you have found a major suit fit.

RESPONDER'S SECOND BID

1. If opener bid the major you were looking for, you have found a major suit fit and placed the opener in the declarer's seat. All there is left to determine is how high your partnership should bid. Since you will be the dummy and you have a major suit fit, you may revalue your hand by adding dummy points (If adding dummy points, no value is given to long cards.) Bid the agreed major to show a fit and your point count. Bid it at the three level to invite game with 8-9 points or at the four level with 10 or more points (you know you have 25 points because he promised at least 15).

2. If opener did not bid the major suit fit you were looking for, tell him your point count by making your rebid in Notrump. Bid 2 Notrump to invite game with 8-9 points or bid 3NT with 10 or more points.

BRIDGE LANGUAGE

If you have located a major suit fit with the opener, a bid of 3 Hearts or 3 Spades says, "We have a fit in this suit and I have 8-9 points. If you have 17 points, put us in game. You may also bid game with 16 points and a five card suit in your hand. Otherwise, pass."

If you have located a major suit fit, a bid of 4 Hearts or 4 Spades says, "We have a fit in this suit and enough points for game. Pass."

If you have not located a major suit fit, a bid of 2 Notrump says, "We do not have a major suit fit, but I have 8-9 points. If you have17 points, bid 3 Notrump. You may also bid 3 Notrump with 16 points and a five card suit in your hand." Use your judgment with 16 points. Pass with 15 points."

If you have not located a major suit fit, a bid if 3 Notrump says, "We do not have a major suit fit but we have enough points for game."

WHAT IF OPENER HAS TWO FOUR CARD MAJORS?

1. If the Notrump opener began with two four card majors and Hearts were not accepted, he knows responder has Spades or he would not have used Stayman. He should correct to Spades at the appropriate level. He bids Spades at the three level if responder bid 2NT and his count is 15 but at the four level if he has 17 points. He may also bid game with 16 points and a five card suit in his hand. If responder bid 3NT, he corrects to 4 Spades.

BRIDGE LANGUAGE

You opened 1 Notrump and partner bid 2 Clubs. You have both majors and bid 2 Hearts. Responder denied Hearts by showing his strength with a 2 Notrump bid. Tell responder, "I also have four Spades and I bid it according to my point count—at the three level with 15 points and at the four level with 16 or 17 points." If responder bid 3 Notrump, jump to 4 Spades. You know you have a fit and enough points for game.

RESPONDER HAS A FOUR CARD MAJOR AND A FIVE CARD MAJOR

Responder used Stayman and opener bid 2 Diamonds denying a four card major. Since his partner's 2 Diamond bid denied a four card major, there is no reason for responder to keep looking for an 4-4 fit in a major suit. Therefore, if responder then bids a major, he began with 5-4 in the majors and is now looking for a 5-3 fit major suit fit. The major is bid at the two level to invite game with 8-9 points or at the three level with 10 or more points.

BRIDGE LANGUAGE

Responder used Stayman and opener denied a four card major by bidding 2 Diamonds. Responder then bid a major suit at the TWO level. He is saying, "I understand you do not have a four card major, but I have 8-9 points and five cards in this major suit. Do you have three? If you do not have three cards, pass with 15 points. Bid 3 Notrump with 17 points. Use your judgment to decide whether or not to go to 3 Notrump with 16 points. If you have three cards, bid four in the major with 17 points. You may also bid four in the major with 16 points and a five card suit in your hand. Otherwise, pass."

Responder used Stayman and opener denied a four card major by bidding 2 Diamonds. Responder then bid a major suit at the THREE level. He is saying, "I understand you do not have a four card major, but I have 10 points and five cards in this suit. Do you have three cards in this suit? If so, bid game in this major suit. If not, bid 3 Notrump."

Ordinarily with 0-7 points, you do not use the Stayman convention. However, because playing a part score contract in a trump fit is safer than passing 1NT, use Stayman with 0-7 points and the following hand distributions; 4 Spades, 4 Hearts, 5 Diamonds and zero Clubs, or 4 Spades, 4 Hearts, 4 Diamonds and one Club. First bid Stayman, then pass any bid the opener makes. You know he is not going to bid Clubs because that is not a response made to Stayman. If he bids Hearts or Spades, you have an eight card fit, if he bids Diamonds, you have either a seven or an eight card fit. By doing this, you rescue the opener from a Notrump contract which is almost doomed to fail. This rarely happens but it is good to know just in case.

The Stayman convention may also be used after an opening 2 Notrump (20-21 HCP's) or opening 2 Club followed by 2 Notrump (22-24 HCP's). An explanation is given following the discussion of Jacoby Transfers.

JACOBY TRANSFERS FOR THE MAJOR SUITS

The Jacoby Transfer convention is designed to help you locate a major suit fit when you hold at least one FIVE card or longer major. Here is how it works. When your partner opens in 1 Notrump, bid the suit below your major suit on the bidding scale. Remember, suits are ranked Clubs, Diamonds, Hearts, and Spades. If your suit is Hearts, bid 2 Diamonds. If your suit is Spades, bid 2 Hearts. This says nothing about the suit you bid. Instead, it requests the opener to bid the suit above it on the bidding scale and is absolutely forcing. Opener must bid the suit you request.

REQUIREMENTS FOR A MAJOR SUIT JACOBY TRANSFER

1. You have at least one FIVE card or longer major.
2. There is no point count requirement for this bid. It may be done with zero points.

Allowing the opener to mention your suit first, places him in the declarer's seat and consequently, opponents will find the hand more difficult to defend. They won't be able to see where the opener's high cards are located and the opening lead will go through the dummy and up to declarer's hand giving declarer a tremendous advantage.

If you have a five or six+ card major, you know you have at least a seven card fit (he promised at least two cards in each suit) but the hand will play better if you place the Notrump opener (the stronger hand) in the declarer's seat. Request the transfer.

PARTNER OPENS 1 NOTRUMP:

A response of 2 Diamonds asks opener to transfer to 2 Hearts. A response of 2 Hearts asks opener to transfer to 2 Spades.

BRIDGE LANGUAGE

In response to 1 Notrump, a bid of 2 Diamonds says, "I have five or more Hearts. Please transfer to my Heart suit. I will tell you the strength of my hand on my next bid."

In response to 1 Notrump, a bid of 2 Hearts says, "I have five or more Spades. Please transfer to my Spade suit. I will tell you the strength of my hand on my next bid."

AFTER OPENER TRANSFERS TO YOUR MAJOR SUIT:

Now, show the strength of your hand:

1. 0–7 points—-Simply pass. You have placed him in a trump suit (at least a seven card fit) and he will be the declarer. This is much safer the passing his 1 Notrump bid. Your weak hand will have some strength because of the trump fit and declarer's hand is hidden from the opponents. You have just done your partner a big favor by rescuing him from the Notrump contract. Feel good about it.

BRIDGE LANGUAGE

You are the opening 1 Notrump bidder and partner responded 2 Diamonds or 2 Hearts. You made the transfer and he passed. He is saying, "We cannot reach game but I have placed you in a trump fit and made you the declarer."

2. 8-9 points and a FIVE card major—-Bid 2NT to invite game.

BRIDGE LANGUAGE

Opener made the requested transfer and responder then bids 2 Notrump. He is saying, "I have 8-9 points and exactly five cards in my suit. If you have 3 cards in my suit, bid a major suit game with a 17 points. You may also bid game with 16 points and a five card suit in your hand. Otherwise, pass. Without three cards, bid 3 Notrump with 17 points. You may also bid game with 16 points and a five card suit in your hand. Otherwise, pass."

Opener made the requested transfer, and then responder bid 3 NT. He is saying, "I have exactly five cards in this suit and 10+ points. Bid 4 in my major with three cards in my suit. Pass 3 Notrump with only two cards in my suit."

3. With a SIX+ card major—Bid your suit to show your suit is longer than five cards. Bid it at the three level to show 8-9 points. Bid it at the 4 level with 10 or more points.

BRIDGE LANGUAGE

Responder requested a transfer and after opener made the transfer, responder raised the suit opener bid. This shows six or more cards. Responder is saying, "I have six cards in my suit. If I bid it at the three level, I have 8-9 points. Bid game in this major with 17 points. You may also bid game with 16 points with a five card suit in your hand. Otherwise, pass."

If after opener has made the transfer, the responder bids game in the transfer suit, he is saying, "I have six or more cards in this suit and 10 or more points. I have no interest in pursuing a slam. Pass."

WHEN RESPONDER HAS TWO FIVE CARD OR LONGER MAJORS

1. First, request a transfer to Spades by bidding Hearts.
2. After the opener makes the transfer to Spades, bid Hearts again to show a five card heart suit. This

shows 5-5 in the majors. If he doesn't have three Spades, he must have three Hearts because he has a balanced hand can have only one doubleton. Opener chooses which of the majors he prefers.

a. The Notrump opener must realize you have five cards in both majors. With 5-4 in the majors, you would have started with Stayman.

BRIDGE LANGUAGE

Responder requested a transfer to Spades by bidding Hearts. After the transfer was made, responder bid Hearts again. He is saying, "I have five cards in both majors. Bid game in the one in which you have 3 cards."

When you first learn Stayman and Jacoby transfers, it is good to keep it simple by just transferring to the major suits. After you become comfortable with major suit transfers, you may want to add minor suit transfers. Until then, when asked if you do transfer bids, just say, "For the major suits only."

MINOR SUIT TRANSFERS

Now that you have added Stayman and major suit transfers to your game, you can sign off at the two level in a major suit with 0-7 points and place opener in the declarer's seat. Until now, you have passed with 0-7 points and no five card major suit. However, if you could take your partner out of the 1Notrump contract and place him in a minor suit contract, his chances would be much better. Minor suit transfers can help you. You can NOT sign off at the two level in either minor suit because now, 2 Clubs is used as Stayman and 2 Diamonds is used as a transfer. But, if your minor suit is at least six cards in length, you may use minor suit transfers to sign off at the three level. Because the transfer is made at a higher level, it is risky but with a guaranteed trump fit, it is usually better than passing 1 Notrump. How do minor suit transfers work?

1. In response to 1 Notrump, bid 2 Spades to request opener to transfer to Clubs at the three level.
   a. After he makes the transfer to 3 Clubs, if Clubs is your long suit, pass.
   b. After he makes the transfer to 3 Clubs, if Diamonds is your long suit, bid 3 Diamonds. Opener must pass as this is a sign off bid.

BRIDGE LANGUAGE

Partner opened 1 Notrump and you have 0-7 points and a six card or longer minor suit. If you bid 2 Spades, you are saying, "I have a weak hand with a long minor suit. Transfer to 3 Clubs and I will pass if my suit is Clubs. If my suit is Diamonds, I will bid 3 Diamonds and you must pass."

There are also major suit Texas Transfer bids. These bids request a transfer but the request is made at game level. For example, in response to 1 Notrump, if responder bids 4 Diamonds he is requesting the opener to transfer to 4 Hearts. If he bids 4 Hearts, he is requesting the opener to transfer to 4 Spades. To make this request responder must have:

a. A six card or longer major.

b. Usually has 8-13 high card points.

c. No interest in slam.

Before you do a Texas transfer, be certain your partner will recognize it. The downside to this bid is that partner may forget he is supposed to transfer. If that happens, you are up a creek without a paddle. It is often a good idea to wait until you are confident in major and minor suit transfers before adding Texas transfers to your game.

Stayman and Jacoby Transfers may also be used after a 2 Notrump opening. There are no invitational responses as partner has already given you his point count and has invited you to game.

RESPONSES TO OPENING 2 NOTRUMP

A. WITH 0-4 POINTS, GAME IS NOT POSSIBLE.
1. Without a five card major suit, pass.
2. With a five card major, you will do partner a big favor if you can place him in a trump contract. Request a transfer and pass his response.

B. WITH 5-11 POINTS, YOU HAVE ENOUGH POINTS FOR GAME.
1. Without a four card or longer major, bid 3 Notrump.

2. Use Stayman with at least one four card major. If you find a fit using Stayman, bid game in that major. With no fit, bid 3 Notrump.

3. With no four card major but you have a five card or longer major(s), request a transfer. After opener makes the transfer, bid game. Bid game in the major with a six card suit. With only a five card suit, bid 3 Notrump and let opener decide if it should be played in a major suit (he has three cards in your suit) or in 3 Notrump (with only two cards).

BRIDGE LANGUAGE

Partner opened with 2 Notrump. If you pass, you are saying, "We do not have enough points for game and I can't help you because I do not have a five card major. Good luck."

Partner opened with 2 Notrump. If you bid 3 Clubs, you are saying, "We have enough points for game. Do you have a four card major?"

Partner opened 2 Notrump. If you bid 2 Diamonds or 2 Hearts, you are saying, "I have a five card or longer major. Please make the transfer. I will tell you my point count on my next bid."

When partner opens in 2 Clubs and then rebids 2 Notrump after your response, this shows a balanced hand with 22-24 points. There are no invitational responses. Partner has already limited his hand and invited you to bid game with enough points. Use Stayman and Jacoby Transfers just as explained above but you need fewer points because his point range is different.

WHAT TO DO WHEN THE OPPONENTS INTERFERE

It is always a problem when the opponents come in to interfere with your Notrump bidding. Unfortunately, partnerships handle it in different ways. This book gives you the Standard American way of coping with interference.

A. Opponents came in and doubled partner's opening Notrump bid.
   1. Make your usual responses including Stayman and transfers. The double has not taken up any space on the bidding scale.
B. Opponents came in and bid a suit immediately over opener's Notrump bid. When you have adopted both the Stayman convention and Jacoby Transfers:
   1. Pass with 0-7 points. The opponent has taken opener out of the Notrump contract and you do not need to rescue him.
   2. The cue bid of the opponent's suit becomes Stayman and is asking if opener has a four card major suit.
   3. Jacoby transfers do not apply. Except for the cue bid of the opponent's suit, all responder's suit bids are natural showing a five card suit and game interest.

4. The bid of a suit (other than opponent's suit) at the two level, shows at least five cards in that suit and eight or nine points. The bid of a suit at the three level, shows five cards in that suit and is forcing to game.

5. The bid of 2Notrump is invitational and 3Notrump is to play.

6. A double is for penalty.

C. Opponent came in over your conventional response (Stayman or Jacoby Transfer) and doubled or bid a suit.

1. Accept your partner's transfer bid with three card support for his suit.

2. Pass with only two cards in partner's suit.

3. Opener may redouble if the opponent doubled if he thinks that is the best contract.

EXERCISES:

Remove a balanced hand with 15-17 points from a deck of cards. Shuffle and deal out the three remaining hands. Referring to the instructions for Stayman and Jacoby transfers, decide how you would respond to a 1Notrump opening bid with each of the hands. Keep shuffling, dealing and responding until you are confident. It takes practice to become proficient.

This concludes basic bidding plus Stayman and Jacoby Transfers. I hope you find this game a great source of enjoyment for your entire lifetime. No matter at what level you eventually play, the basic bidding described in this book will be a solid foundation upon which to build.

As you and your partner (or partners) progress in the game, you will find nothing is etched in stone. You will make exceptions to rules, adjust the point ranges, use more conventions, add other advanced bidding techniques and begin to use judgment. Each change or addition will be exciting. When you discover something new, you will look forward to playing with great anticipation.

GOOD LUCK, GOOD BIDDING AND REMEMBER – ALWAYS BE KIND TO YOUR PARTNER.

Made in the USA
San Bernardino, CA
08 March 2013